Eyes Wide Open

A Weekly Devotional Series for the Busy Woman Wanting to Make Her Moments Count

VOLUME III

by
SHERI EASTER

EYES WIDE OPEN
A Weekly Devotional Series for the Busy Woman Wanting to Make Her Moments Count Volume III
by Sheri Easter

Printed in the United States of America.

ISBN 9781498445016

www.xulonpress.com

ENDORSEMENTS

I know of no one in the gospel music field with more heart or integrity than Sheri Easter. I'm sure that these devotions would certainly spiritually enrich the lives of anyone who reads them.

Bill Gaither

Sheri Easter's voice on paper is as sweet as it is on stage. In this book, she shares her heart and life like a good friend chatting over coffee. Beautiful insights and practical inspiration from someone who has an infectious joy for living and a faith that really can move mountains...and has!

Roberta Croteau
Associate Publisher and Editor In Chief
Homecoming Magazine

Sheri Easter's "Eyes Wide Open" is the busy woman's connection to God!

Each short devotion is a nugget of wisdom followed by powerful Scriptures—it's accessible, encouraging, and faith-building!

Nancy Stafford, Actress ("Matlock", "Christmas with a Capital C"), Speaker, and Author of *The Wonder of His Love: A Journey into the Heart of God* and *Beauty by the Book: Seeing Yourself as God Sees You*

I can remember more than one day while reading Sheri's devotions that my heart was pierced with her words of encouragement.

Her words of wisdom, spoken in love are sure to be a bright spot in your day.

Deon Unthank, CEO/Publisher

AbsolutelyGospel.com

I'm always looking for words of inspiration. The words and messages in this book are some of the most uplifting I have ever read!

Dolly Parton

EYES WIDE OPEN

Now I live with eyes wide open
and my heart is filled with gratitude,
cause I know everything I have is only borrowed
and by the grace of God I know I'll make it through.

From, *I Know How It Feels to Survive*
Sheri Easter/Madison Easter
Copyright 2012

DEDICATION

This series is dedicated to the women in my life who loved deeply, served sacrificially, gave unselfishly, spoke authentically, and laughed with a deep-rooted joy in this wonderful journey we call life…to the ladies who invested in me.

To my beautiful daughters and daughter-in-law, Morgan, Maura and Shannon. You have been blessed by the women before you; love God as they loved God and serve Him and your families with sacrifice, never be afraid to give, speak your heart and laugh with your whole being living each day in the joy of the Lord.

EYES WIDE OPEN – A DEVOTIONAL FOR BUSY WOMEN

--◦⟨≪≫⟩◦--

*T*his devotional is written to inspire you to live a life with eyes wide open, not wanting to miss a moment. It is not intended for reading at a specific time, every day for the next 100 days. Rather it is meant to be a tool whenever you feel the tugging of God beckoning you to have intimacy with him. Many times I've begun those "365 day read your Bible in a year" devotionals and failed. I started out really good with a lot of momentum and somewhere around March; I found myself about 25 days and 150 pages behind with no time to catch up. I felt overwhelmed and I quit.

This book allows you the freedom to pick it up whenever you want encouragement and intimacy with God, then the prayer time and studying is up to you in your own time. I'm not one of those women who wake up and have a morning Bible study at 7 AM just after my morning walk and just before my yoga class. I'm one of those busy women who get up at 5:30 AM to fly out to some far-off destination and then tomorrow morning, I may get up at 7 AM to take my little girl to elementary school. The next day I may choose to sleep in till 10 AM, because I was up until way past midnight and simply need the rest!

Bottom line, this devotional is for busy women – single women busy with careers; busy with school, busy young 'marrieds' trying to make a life for yourself and your husband, young moms trying to raise kids and take care of a job and a household and sometimes everything all at once. This is for the juggling woman. This is for the woman who gets up in the morning and as soon as her feet hit the floor she's off and running.

As godly women, we know we can never be too busy for Him. We must seek Him and spend time with Him, and the only way we can do that in our busy lives is to take every moment and treat it as the precious gift it is – an opportunity to know Him more. I know where He is and I know how to talk to Him, but daily I make a point to spend time with Him.

Make time for God in your schedule. Seek Him. Enjoy discovering what living really is – not just breathing in and breathing out, but living with a heart full of gratitude and eyes wide open!

TABLE OF CONTENTS

DEVOTION 1-MORNING

Last week, Jeff and I were watching an episode of the Andy Griffith Show. It was the one where Andy was a marriage counselor, trying to get a bickering couple to get along. He suggested that they begin each day being nicer to each other by saying, "Morning Dear" and "Morning Honey". So, for a week after that episode; Jeff and I would all day long, in our best Andy voice, say, "Morning Dear", "Morning Honey".

It reminded me of the importance of starting your day in the best way possible. It's Biblical to begin your day with God, but too many of us begin our day with an obnoxious alarm clock, and all day long, we're angry! Some of us start our day with the 'mullygrubs' and even though I'm not certain of the definition or the spelling; I do know what the mullygrubs are!

This week, start your mornings off with God. You may begin by saying "Thank-you" when you open your eyes. God has given you another day! Look at the first person you see, whether it is your spouse, your children or your co-worker and see the beauty in them, thanking God for them being a part of your life. Memorize and quote to yourself, 'morning' scriptures, there are several from which to choose. And trying saying, "Morning Dear"…you never know, someone may reply with "Morning Honey".

Psalm 5:3 (KJV):

3 My voice shalt thou hear in the morning, O Lord; in the morning will I direct my prayer unto thee, and will look up.

Psalm 63:1 (KJV):

1 O God, thou art my God; early will I seek thee: my soul thirsteth for thee, my flesh longeth for thee in a dry and thirsty land, where no water is;

Lamentations 3:22-23 (KJV):

22 It is of the Lord's mercies that we are not consumed, because his compassions fail not.

23 They are new every morning: great is thy faithfulness.

Ezekiel 12:8 (KJV):

8 And in the morning came the word of the Lord unto me, saying,

Isaiah 50:4 (KJV):

4 The Lord God hath given me the tongue of the learned, that I should know how to speak a word in season to him that is weary: he wakeneth morning by morning, he wakeneth mine ear to hear as the learned.

DEVOTION 2-GETTING TO BUSINESS

The Bible offers so much nourishment to the spirit, but it's also full of wisdom for practical, everyday matters in life. It offers parental advice, tips on human relations and even business. Being a business student, I thought I'd share a few Biblical business tips with you, just in case you hadn't found them yet!

Ecclesiastes 11:4 (AMP):

4 He who observes the wind [and waits for all conditions to be favorable] will not sow, and he who regards the clouds will not reap.

Proverbs 6:6-8 (AMP):

6 Go to the ant, you sluggard; consider her ways and be wise! 7 Which, having no chief, overseer, or ruler, 8 Provides her food in the summer and gathers her supplies in the harvest.

Proverbs 10:4-5 (KJV):

4 He becometh poor that dealeth with a slack hand: but the hand of the diligent maketh rich. 5 He that gathereth in summer is a wise son: but he that sleepeth in harvest is a son that causeth shame.

Proverbs 13:11 (NKJV):

11 Wealth gained by dishonesty will be diminished, But he who gathers by labor will increase.

Proverbs 3:9 (TLB):

9-10 Honor the Lord by giving him the first part of all your income, and he will fill your barns with wheat and barley and overflow your wine vats with the finest wines.

Romans 13:6-7 (ESV):

6 For because of this you also pay taxes, for the authorities are ministers of God, attending to this very thing. 7 Pay to all what is owed to them: taxes to whom taxes are owed, revenue to whom revenue is owed, respect to whom respect is owed, honor to whom honor is owed.

Proverbs 31:13-27 (KJV):

13 She seeketh wool, and flax, and worketh willingly with her hands. 14 She is like the merchants' ships; she bringeth her food from afar. 15 She riseth also while it is yet night, and giveth meat to her household, and a portion to her maidens. 16 She considereth a field, and buyeth it: with the fruit of her hands she planteth a vineyard. 17 She girdeth her loins with strength, and strengtheneth her arms. 18 She perceiveth that her merchandise is good: her candle goeth not out by night. 19 She layeth her hands to the spindle, and her hands hold the distaff. 20 She stretcheth out her hand to the poor; yea, she reacheth forth her hands to the needy. 21 She is not afraid of the snow for her household: for all her household are clothed with scarlet. 22 She maketh herself coverings of tapestry; her clothing is silk and purple. 23 Her husband is known in the gates, when he sitteth among the elders of the land. 24 She maketh fine linen, and selleth it; and delivereth girdles unto the merchant. 25 Strength and honour are her clothing; and she shall rejoice in time to come. 26 She openeth her mouth with wisdom; and in her tongue is the law of kindness. 27 She looketh well to the ways of her household, and eateth not the bread of idleness.

DEVOTION 3-SPRING-CLEANING

When I hear the very first bird chirp as winter is passing, my mind immediately goes to spring-cleaning! There is something so freeing about getting all of the clutter out of your life and giving your house a good scrubbing. I like to organize, in fact, I can't prove this, but I'll bet the teacher gave me stars when it came to putting like with like. My idea of life is that everything has a place and everything *should* be in it! For all of you judging, make certain you read my disclaimer!

The Bible has a few things to say about spring-cleaning, too! It tells us to keep our heart clean, renew our mind, be cleansed from a guilty conscience and wash with pure water! Spring-cleaning your home may only last a short while, but keeping your heart and mind clean will last an eternity.

The most wonderful thing about spring-cleaning—of the house and of the heart—is the attitude that comes with the results! When you remove all of the dirt, dust and clutter, you respond differently to everything in your life. It is as if the weight of the world has been lifted and your eyes have been opened to something new and fresh. With a renewing of your mind and spirit, you can begin to bring order to the tasks you face in life!

Psalm 51:10 (KJV):

10 10 Create in me a clean heart, O God; and renew a right spirit within me.

Hebrews 10:22 (NIV):

22 Let us draw near to God with a sincere heart and with the full assurance that faith brings, having our hearts sprinkled to cleanse us from a guilty conscience and having our bodies washed with pure water.

Ephesians 4:31-32 (NIV):

31 Get rid of all bitterness, rage and anger, brawling and slander, along with every form of malice. 32 Be kind and compassionate to one another, forgiving each other, just as in Christ God forgave you.

1 Corinthians 14:40 (NIV):

40 But everything should be done in a fitting and orderly way.

DEVOTION 4-HOPE IN CHRIST

I've been thinking a lot this week about our trip to Israel a few years ago. I remember so vividly when 'the city set on a hill' first came into view. I was enamored with it at first sight—the streets where Jesus walked, the sacred ground I had read about since I was a child.

I remember sitting in the gardens in front of the tomb with Golgotha's hill in view and trying to imagine the hopelessness the disciples must have felt. Maybe it compared to the hopelessness I have felt before, when my Daddy died, when I was diagnosed with breast cancer, or when my Mama became bedridden with Parkinson's? Maybe it compared to the hopelessness you have felt before, with the death of a spouse, or your child?

I do know this; hopelessness is big, it looms and it smothers! I'm sure if the disciples could have hoped through Calvary to the empty tomb; Christ's death wouldn't have felt so overwhelmingly final. This week, whatever you may be facing, remember that in three short days, the disciples and family of Christ went from hopelessness to hopeful— from devastation to celebration, from defeat to victory! Because of the cross and the tomb, you have a hope in Christ!

Matthew 27:45-46 (NIV):
The Death of Jesus

45 From noon until three in the afternoon darkness came over all the land. 46 About three in the afternoon Jesus cried out in a loud voice, "Eli, Eli, lema sabachthani?" (which means "My God, my God, why have you forsaken me?").

Mark 16:5-7 (NIV):

5 As they entered the tomb, they saw a young man dressed in a white robe sitting on the right side, and they were alarmed.6 "Don't be alarmed," he said. "You are looking for Jesus the

Nazarene, who was crucified. He has risen! He is not here. See the place where they laid him. 7 But go, tell his disciples and Peter, 'He is going ahead of you into Galilee. There you will see him, just as he told you.'"

Luke 24:6-7 (NIV):

6 He is not here; he has risen! Remember how he told you, while he was still with you in Galilee: 7 'The Son of Man must be delivered over to the hands of sinners, be crucified and on the third day be raised again.' "

1 Corinthians 15:55-57 (NIV):

55 "Where, O death, is your victory? Where, O death, is your sting?" 56 The sting of death is sin, and the power of sin is the law. 57 But thanks be to God! He gives us the victory through our Lord Jesus Christ.

DEVOTION 5-CHOOSE THEM CAREFULLY

Last week, I read a quote that I had said in an interview about 25 years ago. I responded with a statement that whether it's the message in our songs or Jeff's humor, or even a smile that encourages them; I like to see people leave our concerts a little differently than they came. It was a very simple, but earnest expression from my heart, but it obviously was very effective at describing what 'Jeff & Sheri Easter' are all about, because it has been printed hundreds of times in magazines or in bios, and it has been quoted in radio interviews and introductions…it resonated with people and they remember!

Grandma always said to choose your words carefully, I read somewhere later the little phrase "and make them sweet…in case you have to eat them." It's really true! Your words will come back to you, bitter or sweet, because people remember. Let them come back as a testament to your kindness, or your sincerity, or maybe even your great sense of humor. Don't say things that will be a testament to your lack of self-esteem, your bitterness or selfishness, your piety or critical spirit. Trust me, your words do linger, sometimes for years, choose them carefully…and just in case, it wouldn't hurt to make them sweet!

1 Thessalonians 5:11 (KJV):

11 Wherefore comfort yourselves together, and edify one another, even as also ye do.

Romans 14:19 (KJV):

19 Let us therefore follow after the things which make for peace, and things wherewith one may edify another.

Ephesians 4:29 (KJV):

29 Let no corrupt communication proceed out of your mouth, but that which is good to the use of edifying, that it may minister grace unto the hearers.

Proverbs 10:11 (KJV):

11 The mouth of a righteous man is a well of life: but violence covereth the mouth of the wicked.

Proverbs 25:11 (KJV):

11 A word fitly spoken is like apples of gold in pictures of silver.

DEVOTION 6-HONOR

The word "honor" means to respect, admire or look up to. It has been my privilege for over fifty years now to honor my mother. She is the most loving, kind, joyful, caring and peace-filled woman I have ever known. I wrote the song, *She Loved*, about her several years ago and it was such a personal message that I never thought I would record or perform it. I'm so glad I did.

The song has resonated with so many people who know women who know how to love. It is written for women who are faithful wives…Mama was married to my Daddy for twenty-four years. Eight years after Daddy died, she remarried and was again, a faithful wife to Leon for 21 years. It is written for sacrificial mothers; Mama always put my little brother and me, and our needs before hers. It is written to celebrate women who served God with every fiber of their being, praying, teaching, giving and living every moment according to His divine leadership.

As I honor Mama, by sharing her with each of you, think about the very special women in your lives and honor them this week. Tell them thank you, even though it seems inadequate, hug them a little tighter, and say "I love you." As a mama myself; I can assure you, there are no sweeter words to hear!

Exodus 20:12 (KJV):

12 Honour thy father and thy mother: that thy days may be long upon the land which the Lord thy God giveth thee.

Deuteronomy 5:16 (KJV):

16 Honour thy father and thy mother, as the Lord thy God hath commanded thee; that thy days may be prolonged, and that it may go well with thee, in the land which the Lord thy God giveth thee.

Ephesians 6:2 (KJV):

2 Honour thy father and mother; which is the first commandment with promise;

Romans 12:10 (KJV):

10 Be kindly affectioned one to another with brotherly love; in honour preferring one another;

DEVOTION 7-WHAT IS BEST?

Prioritizing is one of the hardest jobs of a Christian, simply because there are so many good choices that you could make in a given day. Especially if you're a wife; a mother, a worker, a servant, an encourager, a caregiver, an instructor and some-times all of the above in the course of twenty-four hours. How do we determine *what is best?*

The Bible gives us a wonderful story of Mary and Martha, and I've admitted publicly that I battle against my *Martha* ten-dencies, but it also gives us other wonderful scriptures that help us spend our time wisely. I remember when Jeff and I first married; I was so excited to be his wife and I wanted to spoil him with my attention. One of the things I did was pack his clothes each week. I did that for three years...until Madison was born. Honestly, I would have continued packing for him, but in the three 24-hour days I was home some weeks; I barely had time to wash the clothes, clean the house, and pay the bills, let alone pack the diapers, wipes, bottles, bottle brush, steril-izer, pacifier, 3 changes of clothes per day, bibs, socks, shoes, toys, medical bag, Q-tips, baby shampoo, washcloths, towels, pajamas...(wow, I'm tired just remembering having to do all of that!) Time wasn't my friend.

And it never is. Be assured that you are given only so much time. You must make wise decisions about how to spend it. Do you want to work non-stop while your family waits for you to join them? Do you want to spend your precious moments arguing about things that aren't important? Do you want to listen to someone ramble on about politics or theology or how miserable their lives are when instead you could say a prayer for them, then trust that God and His Holy Spirit is in control?

This week spend your time wisely; pray for your needs and the needs of your family and friends. There are only so many hours in a day and the choice belongs to you. My DEVOTION is done, my little girl has curled up on the sofa with me and now it's time for me to wrap my arms around her because *that, my friends, is best!*

Psalm 90:12 (TLB):

12 Teach us to number our days and recognize how few they are; help us to spend them as we should.

Luke 10:42 (KJV):

42 But one thing is needful: and Mary hath chosen that good part, which shall not be taken away from her.

Colossians 4:5 (KJV):

5 Walk in wisdom toward them that are without, redeeming the time.

Proverbs 31:15-18 (TLB):

15 She gets up before dawn to prepare breakfast for her household and plans the day's work for her servant girls. 16 She goes out to inspect a field and buys it; with her own hands she plants a vineyard. 17 She is energetic, a hard worker, 18 and watches for bargains. She works far into the night!

Psalm 31:15 (TLB):

14-15 But I am trusting you, O Lord. I said, "You alone are my God; my times are in your hands. Rescue me from those who hunt me down relentlessly.

DEVOTION 8-20/20 VISION

I've been very blessed to have 20/20 vision all my life. In fact, a couple of years ago, my doctor prescribed reading glasses because obviously; I'm getting older, yet he stressed that I still had 20/20 vision. That threw me a bit, so I researched and found that 20/20 vision refers to your ability to see at 20 feet clearly what a normal person should be able to see at 20 feet. It doesn't necessarily mean 'perfect' vision, but just the quality or sharpness of vision at a distance.

Sometimes in life, we 'see' what is around us, just maybe not as clearly as we should. Maybe it's not clear, because we're focused on something else that simply robs us of what we could see if we had such a thing as 'perfect' vision rather than 20/20. That's why it's so important to walk by faith and not necessarily by sight. Because we don't have perfect vision, we must rely on Someone who does.

Just as a seeing eye dog has the job of conveying to someone blind, the possible dangers ahead; God offers His Holy Spirit to lead and guide us when our way simply isn't clear. He promised He would never leave us or forsake us because we needed that promise. When our way isn't clear, we can trust His promise to lead.

2 Corinthians 5:6-8 (KJV):

6 Therefore we are always confident, knowing that, whilst we are at home in the body, we are absent from the Lord: 7 (For we walk by faith, not by sight:) 8 We are confident, I say, and willing rather to be absent from the body, and to be present with the Lord.

John 3:5-8 (KJV):

5 Jesus answered, Verily, verily, I say unto thee, Except a man be born of water and of the Spirit, he cannot enter into the kingdom of God. 6 That which is born of the flesh is flesh; and that which is born of the Spirit is spirit. 7 Marvel not that I said unto thee, Ye must be born again. 8 The wind bloweth where it listeth, and thou hearest the sound thereof, but canst not tell whence it cometh, and whither it goeth: so is every one that is born of the Spirit.

Hebrews 13:5-6 (KJV):

5 Let your conversation be without covetousness; and be content with such things as ye have: for he hath said, I will never leave thee, nor forsake thee. 6 So that we may boldly say, The Lord is my helper, and I will not fear what man shall do unto me.

DEVOTION 9-BACK TO BASICS

I like to sing about everyday life. I like to sing about God's mercies being new every morning, about His faithfulness in my life, about the blessings He's given me...everyday life! These are the kinds of things that I think about every day, because this is where I live every day, but as a singer; I have to remember, not everyone lives where I do everyday. Some people don't realize that His mercy is new every morning or that He is faithful and maybe some don't even know that they are blessed, so it's my job to sing a message that touches people 'where they live.'

Where do you live? Have you accepted Christ as your Savior? Have you read and believed John 3:16? If so, have you surrendered your life to serve God? Do you even know how to serve Him?

Every time I find myself seeking for answers that only God can give, I go back to His word. I spend time searching the stories, learning about the interesting characters, seeing their faults and failures and remembering that in spite of my faults and failures, God loves me. I think when we all get back to the basics of Christianity; we simply remember that He loves us, and wherever we 'live' today, isn't that the greatest thing to remember?

John 3:16 (KJV):

16 For God so loved the world, that he gave his only begotten Son, that whosoever believeth in him should not perish, but have everlasting life.

Romans 5:8 (KJV):

8 But God commendeth his love toward us, in that, while we were yet sinners, Christ died for us.

Ephesians 2:4-5 (KJV):

4 But God, who is rich in mercy, for his great love wherewith he loved us, 5 Even when we were dead in sins, hath quickened us together with Christ, (by grace ye are saved;)

1 John 4:9-11 (KJV):

9 In this was manifested the love of God toward us, because that God sent his only begotten Son into the world, that we might live through him. 10 Herein is love, not that we loved God, but that he loved us, and sent his Son to be the propitiation for our sins.

11 Beloved, if God so loved us, we ought also to love one another.

Proverbs 8:17 (KJV):

17 I love them that love me; and those that seek me early shall find me.

DEVOTION 10-PAPER AND INK

I cleaned out a closet this week! This was no ordinary closet. This was the closet that held hundreds of 'Thinking of You' and 'Get Well' cards when I went through breast cancer six years ago this summer. I've tried to do it many times before, but when I started touching those cards, those precious words of encouragement, those prayers from people who loved me enough to say it with the written word—I just couldn't. So there they sat, taking up about four feet by three feet of my closet space.

This week I was reminded that although those tangible expressions of love carried me through a very difficult year, they're just paper and ink...the love in the cards is in my heart! So, I decided it was time. As I bagged up the last of the cards, I held the bag and prayed, knowing that some of the senders are struggling today, some are celebrating today and some are no longer with us. I prayed for my senders and their families with gratefulness that they prayed for me.

It's okay to let go; in fact it's healthy. The Bible says to store up your treasures in heaven where neither moth nor rust will decay. It's time to get rid of some of the clutter in your life, knowing that the love that was attached will live on in your heart! You really don't need the paper and ink to remind you of that, do you?

Matthew 6:19-21 (KJV):

19 Lay not up for yourselves treasures upon earth, where moth and rust doth corrupt, and where thieves break through and steal: 20 But lay up for yourselves treasures in heaven, where neither moth nor rust doth corrupt, and where thieves do not break through nor steal: 21 For where your treasure is, there will your heart be also.

Colossians 3:2 (KJV):

2 Set your affection on things above, not on things on the earth.

DEVOTION 11-REMIND ME AGAIN

I love the way people treat each other when a baby is born, or when a loved one passes away. I love the way people hug and speak kindness to moms on Mother's Day or the way they post pictures of dads on Father's Day. I love the way folks go out of their way to be at birthday parties or graduations, just to say, "I love you" or "I'm proud of you." It's a shame we can't remember to live this way everyday.

I really think a lot of us would if we only remembered to. We forget the sharpness of our tongue or we're too distracted to pay attention to someone we love. Thank goodness for birthdays, graduations, births, deaths, and holidays. They make us stop and remember. Remember to be kind, remember to show our love and remember to extend a helping hand to someone who is hurting. They remind us to be more like Jesus.

Take time this week to remember and ask God to remind you again how He wants you to love others.

1 John 4:7-9 (KJV):

7 Beloved, let us love one another: for love is of God; and every one that loveth is born of God, and knoweth God. 8 He that loveth not knoweth not God; for God is love.

9 In this was manifested the love of God toward us, because that God sent his only begotten Son into the world, that we might live through him.

Ephesians 6:2 (KJV):

2 Honour thy father and mother; which is the first commandment with promise;

DEVOTION 12-WAIT

Every week, I begin praying and asking God; what is it that I need to write about? This week has been a very busy week, beginning with bus repairs and ending with Jeff's knee surgery all wrapped up in the title, 'vacation' since we didn't work this weekend. Not exactly the 'vacation' I would hope for, but it's been a time of gratitude, time with my family, but also, some time spent waiting...waiting for the bus, waiting for Jeff's healing! It made me think of the scripture that I found a few years ago while trying to make a major career decision.

I've never been much for patience. I move at lightning speed and run until I drop! My career choice is famous for it's 'hurry up and wait' and sometimes, so is life. We start out at breakneck speeds, anxious to see our dreams and desires come to pass; day after day, week after week, month after month and sometimes year after year...it seems to get a little harder when you find yourself waiting longer than what your original calendar would have hoped.

The thing about waiting is that it gives you time to prepare, time to learn, time to adjust, and time to experience. So if you're feeling like God has forgotten your dream, simply because you're still waiting, be reminded of these scriptures and trust Him while you wait!

Proverbs 19:2 (NRSV):

2 Desire without knowledge is not good, and one who moves too hurriedly misses the way.

Habakkuk 2:3 (MSG): Full of Self, but Soul-Empty

2-3 And then God answered: "Write this. Write what you see. Write it out in big block letters so that it can be read on the run. This vision-message is a witness pointing to what's coming. It aches for the coming—it can hardly wait! And it doesn't lie. If it seems slow in coming, wait. It's on its way. It will come right on time.

DEVOTION 13-A
TEACHABLE SPIRIT

I've always loved teachers. I am a teacher's pet! I like to absorb every bit of knowledge that I can from teachers. I LOVE to learn...anything from history to current affairs, decorating to construction, or science to trivia. I'm like a sponge and whenever I have the opportunity to be with teachers, I listen.

The Bible tells us that Jesus is a teacher. If we take time to listen to what His words are teaching, we can learn how to be our best. Maintain a teachable spirit throughout this week and learn what it is that God wants you to learn. He's always present, always teaching, your only job is to listen.

Matthew 5:2 (KJV):

2 And he opened his mouth, and taught them, saying,

Mark 6:34 (KJV):

34 And Jesus, when he came out, saw much people, and was moved with compassion toward them, because they were as sheep not having a shepherd: and he began to teach them many things.

Luke 5:3 (KJV):

3 And he entered into one of the ships, which was Simon's, and prayed him that he would thrust out a little from the land. And he sat down, and taught the people out of the ship.

John 3:2 (KJV):

2 The same came to Jesus by night, and said unto him, Rabbi, we know that thou art a teacher come from God: for no man can do these miracles that thou doest, except God be with him.

John 8:2 (KJV):

2 And early in the morning he came again into the temple, and all the people came unto him; and he sat down, and taught them.

John 7:16 (NIV):

16 Jesus answered, "My teaching is not my own. It comes from the one who sent me.

2 John 1:9 (NIV):

9 Anyone who runs ahead and does not continue in the teaching of Christ does not have God; whoever continues in the teaching has both the Father and the Son.

DEVOTION 14-JUST TOO MUCH

Some days it's just too much—too much confusion, too much stress, too much to handle, simply too much! We want to throw up our hands and surrender; we just don't have any more fight left in us. So how do we find our fight again, how do we find a better attitude to keep going? I think we look at Peter, or maybe David, perhaps Job...

This week has been too much! At the risk of sounding like I'm complaining, we had three breakdowns in four days, traveled over two thousand miles in four different vehicles (each consecutively growing smaller), encountered slow-moving trains and fast-moving bees, and did twice the job with half of our work force. I'm tired, I haven't slept more than four hours in the past twenty-nine and it's just too much. I need a little help from someone who's been there, someone who knows how I feel.

If we look at Peter, David and Job, they knew where to turn when life became too much. They turned to God because He had the compassion they needed, the understanding they needed, the wisdom, the patience and love they needed...He had—just enough!

Matthew 14:28-31 (NIV):

28 "Lord, if it's you," Peter replied, "tell me to come to you on the water." 29 "Come," he said. Then Peter got down out of the boat, walked on the water and came toward Jesus. 30 But when he saw the wind, he was afraid and, beginning to sink, cried out, "Lord, save me!" 31 Immediately Jesus reached out his hand and caught him. "You of little faith," he said, "why did you doubt?"

Psalm 142 (KJV):

142 I cried unto the Lord with my voice; with my voice unto the Lord did I make my supplication. 2 I poured out my complaint before him; I shewed before him my trouble.

3 When my spirit was overwhelmed within me, then thou knewest my path. In the way wherein I walked have they privily laid a snare for me. 4 I looked on my right hand, and beheld, but there was no man that would know me: refuge failed me; no man cared for my soul. 5 I cried unto thee, O Lord: I said, Thou art my refuge and my portion in the land of the living. 6 Attend unto my cry; for I am brought very low: deliver me from my persecutors; for they are stronger than I. 7 Bring my soul out of prison, that I may praise thy name: the righteous shall compass me about; for thou shalt deal bountifully with me.

Job 1:9-11 (KJV):

9 Then Satan answered the Lord, and said, Doth Job fear God for nought? 10 Hast not thou made an hedge about him, and about his house, and about all that he hath on every side? thou hast blessed the work of his hands, and his substance is increased in the land.

11 But put forth thine hand now, and touch all that he hath, and he will curse thee to thy face.

Job 1:20-22 (KJV):

20 Then Job arose, and rent his mantle, and shaved his head, and fell down upon the ground, and worshipped,

21 And said, Naked came I out of my mother's womb, and naked shall I return thither: the Lord gave, and the Lord hath taken away; blessed be the name of the Lord. 22 In all this Job sinned not, nor charged God foolishly.

Job 22:5 (KJV):

5 Is not thy wickedness great? and thine iniquities infinite?

Job 42:10-17 (KJV):

10 And the Lord turned the captivity of Job, when he prayed for his friends: also the Lord gave Job twice as much as he had before. 11 Then came there unto him all his brethren, and all his sisters, and all they that had been of his acquaintance before, and did eat bread with him in his house: and they bemoaned him, and comforted him over all the evil that the Lord had brought upon him: every man also gave him a piece of money, and every one an earring of gold. 12 So the Lord blessed the latter end of Job more than his beginning: for he had fourteen thousand sheep, and six thousand camels, and a thousand yoke of oxen, and a thousand she asses. 13 He had also seven sons and three daughters.

14 And he called the name of the first, Jemima; and the name of the second, Kezia; and the name of the third, Kerenhappuch. 15 And in all the land were no women found so fair as the daughters of Job: and their father gave them inheritance among their brethren.

16 After this lived Job an hundred and forty years, and saw his sons, and his sons' sons, even four generations. 17 So Job died, being old and full of days.

DEVOTION 15-PRAISE GOD ANYWAY

After having a few tough weeks of travel; I've been thinking a lot about keeping my focus on God, instead of my circumstances. Many times that's where we go wrong with our thinking patterns. We try to figure out how something is going to work out or what we can do to make something happen differently, when in truth, we should instead be thinking on things that are lovely; things that are pure, things that are of good report, trusting that God is more than able to meet all of our needs.

I came across this scripture in Habakkuk that summed up someone being very much in need, very close to hitting bottom, but reminding himself of praising God anyway and it reminded me to do the same. This week, if you're struggling, immediately stop and thank God for your blessings. If you're hurting, thank God for healing, and if you're feeling like giving up, keep going! Through all of the circumstances you face, praise God anyway!

Philippians 4:8 (KJV):

8 Finally, brethren, whatsoever things are true, whatsoever things are honest, whatsoever things are just, whatsoever things are pure, whatsoever things are lovely, whatsoever things are of good report; if there be any virtue, and if there be any praise, think on these things.

Habakkuk 3:17-18 (NIV):

17 Though the fig tree does not bud and there are no grapes on the vines, though the olive crop fails and the fields produce no food, though there are no sheep in the pen and no cattle in the stalls, 18 yet I will rejoice in the Lord, I will be joyful in God my Savior.

DEVOTION 16-THE ACT OF SERVICE

Life can be tough on any given day. When you go through struggles or hardships, one way to forget about your troubles is to remember to give service to others. The Bible has many verses encouraging us to serve one another.

We live in a day where few are willing to serve without knowing "what's in it for me." Service is about forgetting 'you' and thinking of others. We've been very blessed over these past few weeks by people who have forgotten their own troubles and remembered to pray for us. We've had friends act in servant hood by loaning us vehicles to make our dates. And we've continued to act in service to those around us because we know that it is what God expects of us.

Every day this week, do one act of service for someone. Volunteer to buy someone's groceries for them, offer to mow someone's lawn, take someone out for a meal or put gas in someone's vehicle. Just do something to serve, and for a little while, forget about you!

Luke 22:27 (KJV):

27 For whether is greater, he that sitteth at meat, or he that serveth? is not he that sitteth at meat? but I am among you as he that serveth.

Philippians 2:7 (KJV):

7 But made himself of no reputation, and took upon him the form of a servant, and was made in the likeness of men:

2 Corinthians 4:5 (KJV):

5 For we preach not ourselves, but Christ Jesus the Lord; and ourselves your servants for Jesus' sake.

Galatians 5:13 (KJV):

13 For, brethren, ye have been called unto liberty; only use not liberty for an occasion to the flesh, but by love serve one another.

DEVOTION 17-ONE BREATH AT A TIME

When I was a teenager, my Mama loved to sing the song; "One Day At A Time." She sang it onstage and off. It became a kind of mantra for her, as she walked through each season of her life, trusting God was taking care of her every need. It was her reminder that she could do nothing for her circumstances except trust Him. She sang it after my Daddy died, leaving her a widow raising two children who still lived at home. She sang it as she walked through every lonely day until she remarried. She sang it as her husband battled cancer, and as her parents passed away thirteen months apart. She sang it as she walked into the uncertainty of Parkinson's disease.

I never understood her attachment to the song until I began walking through similar seasons. Some days are just too hard. Some fights are just not worth it. Sometimes you need to be reminded that God is taking care of your every need. Nevertheless, I think my mantra will be a little different, because some days I don't have the strength to walk 'one day at a time', and not even one hour or one minute at a time. I think I'll make a conscience effort to trust God one breath at a time!

1 Chronicles 16:11 (KJV):

11 Seek the Lord and his strength, seek his face continually.

Isaiah 41:10 (KJV):

10 Fear thou not; for I am with thee: be not dismayed; for I am thy God: I will strengthen thee; yea, I will help thee; yea, I will uphold thee with the right hand of my righteousness.

Hebrews 11:1 (KJV):

1 Now faith is the substance of things hoped for, the evidence of things not seen.

Jeremiah 17:5 (NIV):

5 This is what the Lord says: "Cursed is the one who trusts in man, who draws strength from mere flesh and whose heart turns away from the Lord.

Job 33:4 (NIV):

4 The Spirit of God has made me; the breath of the Almighty gives me life.

DEVOTION 18-REPAY EVIL WITH KINDNESS

We've all been there—tried to do what God has called us to do and met with criticism and opposition, harsh remarks and mocking. Sometimes it makes you question what you know in your heart to be true. Whenever you feel someone has treated you unfairly, don't be so quick to get even. Instead turn your focus to God. He promises to avenge you.

This week if someone insults you or hurts your feelings, repay their evil with blessing so that you will inherit a blessing. Don't try to get revenge, but instead repay their evil with kindness.

1 Peter 3:9 (NIV):

9 Do not repay evil with evil or insult with insult. On the contrary, repay evil with blessing, because to this you were called so that you may inherit a blessing.

Romans 12:17-21 (NIV):

17 Do not repay anyone evil for evil. Be careful to do what is right in the eyes of everyone. 18 If it is possible, as far as it depends on you, live at peace with everyone. 19 Do not take revenge, my dear friends, but leave room for God's wrath, for it is written: "It is mine to avenge; I will repay," says the Lord. 20 On the contrary: "If your enemy is hungry, feed him; if he is thirsty, give him something to drink. In doing this, you will heap burning coals on his head." 21 Do not be overcome by evil, but overcome evil with good.

Proverbs 17:13 (NIV):

13 Evil will never leave the house of one who pays back evil for good.

DEVOTION 19-FORGOTTEN

Have you ever felt forgotten, left out, unimportant? I met a young girl recently who was absolutely beautiful...beautiful face and a beautiful spirit, you couldn't help noticing her, but she felt forgotten. Life had given her a set of circumstances, her reality that left her in a place where no one noticed her. Her sibling required around-the-clock care, from her, her parents, her family, her friends and most strangers as well. And she felt forgotten.

You may not have this same set of circumstances, but we've all felt at some point that everyone had forgotten us. We wait patiently to be remembered or maybe even do something out of the ordinary, maybe even opposite of our nature, just to be noticed. The Bible says that even though a mother may forget her child, God cannot forget us. I just wanted to remind you today that He has not forgotten!

Luke 12:6-7 (NIV):

6 Are not five sparrows sold for two pennies? Yet not one of them is forgotten by God. 7 Indeed, the very hairs of your head are all numbered. Don't be afraid; you are worth more than many sparrows.

Isaiah 49:15-16 (NIV):

15 "Can a mother forget the baby at her breast and have no compassion on the child she has borne? Though she may forget, I will not forget you! 16 See, I have engraved you on the palms of my hands; your walls are ever before me.

Hebrews 6:10 (NIV):

10 God is not unjust; he will not forget your work and the love you have shown him as you have helped his people and continue to help them.

DEVOTION 20-TRY WALKING TWO

It hurts me to see so much *apathy* these days, maybe there's more or maybe, through social media, we just have more access to it, but it seems to be everywhere! I remember hearing the word for the first time in my English class and trying to understand how someone could simply have no feelings about something, no caring, no understanding, nothing! But it appears to be more common every day.

As upsetting as apathy is in the world, in the church it's even more upsetting to see a lack of *sympathy* these days. I remember a time, when someone could share with church members what they were going through and although the folks may have never experienced it themselves, they showed sympathy for the hurting family by calling, visiting, or sending a card or a casserole. They were quick to show the family that they cared.

Which brings us to the third word; *empathy*, walking through something someone else has walked through and understanding his or her pain. When you are empathetic with someone, they draw healing and strength from your journey, it is an encouragement simply because you understand how they feel. As Christians, although we may not be able to have empathy for everyone because all of our circumstances may be very different, but we can always choose to have sympathy to show them we care. Remember the old adage, to understand a man's journey, 'walk a mile in his shoes'; maybe this week we could try walking two!

1 Peter 3:8 (NKJV):

Called to Blessing

8 Finally, all of you be of one mind, having compassion for one another; love as brothers, be tenderhearted, be courteous;

Romans 12:15 (NKJV):

15 Rejoice with those who rejoice, and weep with those who weep.

1 John 3:17 (NKJV):

17 But whoever has this world's goods, and sees his brother in need, and shuts up his heart from him, how does the love of God abide in him?

DEVOTION 21-PRAISE HIS NAME

Jeff and I took a little two-day vacation this week, just because! It was wonderful to feel the sand between my toes and hear the majesty of the waves pounding against the shore. I try to always see God in everything, but for me; He's even more evident in the mountains or by the seas.

While I was there, I received a phone call from a friend who just wanted to remind me of what a great song *Praise His Name* still is. After twenty years, it's still surfacing into the sales charts. I started thinking about it and its message; it is sacred, it is respect, it is honor, something we lack severely in the culture in which we live.

We have forgotten holiness. Take time this week to be holy. Spend time in praise, worship and adoration of a holy God. Find sacredness and praise His name.

Psalm 100:1-5 (KJV):

1 Make a joyful noise unto the Lord, all ye lands. 2 Serve the Lord with gladness: come before his presence with singing. 3 Know ye that the Lord he is God: it is he that hath made us, and not we ourselves; we are his people, and the sheep of his pasture.

4 Enter into his gates with thanksgiving, and into his courts with praise: be thankful unto him, and bless his name. 5 For the Lord is good; his mercy is everlasting; and his truth endureth to all generations.

Psalm 99:1-9 (KJV):

1 The Lord reigneth; let the people tremble: he sitteth between the cherubims; let the earth be moved. 2 The Lord is great in Zion; and he is high above all the people. 3 Let them praise thy great and terrible name; for it is holy. 4 The king's strength also loveth judgment; thou dost establish equity, thou executest judgment and righteousness in

Jacob. 5 Exalt ye the Lord our God, and worship at his footstool; for he is holy. 6 Moses and Aaron among his priests, and Samuel among them that call upon his name; they called upon the Lord, and he answered them. 7 He spake unto them in the cloudy pillar: they kept his testimonies, and the ordinance that he gave them. 8 Thou answeredst them, O Lord our God: thou wast a God that forgavest them, though thou tookest vengeance of their inventions. 9 Exalt the Lord our God, and worship at his holy hill; for the Lord our God is holy.

DEVOTION 22-THEY ARE WEAK, BUT HE IS STRONG

I was thinking this morning about the enduring power of such a simple song like *Jesus Loves Me*. One of the reasons I believe it continues to inspire is its appeal to children. I've always said that a song will be a hit if the children love it. There is something about their honesty or innocence that hears the true message.

Maybe it's the lifting up of Jesus' name. He promises that He'll draw all men when He is lifted, and His promises are something we can always count on.

Then again, it may be as simple as our acknowledgment of our weakness and His strength. It's nice to know that when we can't; He can. It comforts us to know that when our abilities aren't enough, His are more than enough. His strength is made perfect in our weakness. We can glory in our weaknesses knowing that the power of Christ rests upon us. We may be weak, but He is strong.

Mark 10:15-16 (KJV):

15 Verily I say unto you, Whosoever shall not receive the kingdom of God as a little child, he shall not enter therein. 16 And he took them up in his arms, put his hands upon them, and blessed them.

John 12:32 (KJV):

32 And I, if I be lifted up from the earth, will draw all men unto me.

2 Corinthians 12:9-10 (KJV):

9 And he said unto me, My grace is sufficient for thee: for my strength is made perfect in weakness. Most gladly therefore will I rather glory in my infirmities, that the power of Christ may rest upon me. 10 Therefore I take pleasure in infirmities, in reproaches, in necessities, in persecutions, in distresses for Christ's sake: for when I am weak, then am I strong.

DEVOTION 23-NO CHARGE

Today ,Jeff and I were sitting out at a beautiful seaside restaurant having a delicious lunch, when I looked at him and said, "Isn't it amazing that God has allowed us to be a part of this wonderful cruise so far away from home and someone else has paid the expense for us to be here?" One of the blessings of this incredible 'job' that I have is sometimes our expenses are covered ahead of time and this was one of those times.

All I could think of is how often God blesses us with far greater than what we really deserve, the greatest of these gifts being salvation. He allowed us to be a part of His wonderful family and paid the price for us. When the debts were added and all our sins accounted for, we heard the words, "No charge, the price has already been paid."

John 3:16 (KJV):

16 For God so loved the world, that he gave his only begotten Son, that whosoever believeth in him should not perish, but have everlasting life.

Romans 5:8 (KJV):

8 But God commendeth his love toward us, in that, while we were yet sinners, Christ died for us.

DEVOTION 24-BROTHERLY LOVE

This week as we flew back into Atlanta, we had a two hour layover in Philadelphia. I immediately thought of its name, The City of Brotherly Love. It made me remember the last time I saw a wonderful example of brotherly love. I hate to say this, but it's not as often as I remember it once was.

I've been known to scroll through a Facebook feed and just cry at some of the hurtful things people are saying to each other. People calling out others' sins or bad behavior forget that those of us who know THEM know the sins or bad behavior for which they have been forgiven. It's as if we have forgotten how to really love each other and be kind. One of my favorite Mother Teresa quotes is, "If you judge people, you have no time to love them."

Our little town is reeling after the death of one it's five thousand. A young, beautiful, fifty-two year old mother of two sons, with a smile that could light up a room, slipped away two weeks ago after an eight month battle with cancer. At Christmas last year, Mama was bedridden going on two years, while Laura was healthy as far as any of us knew. In less than a year, we were mourning her death, but remembering her heart. Please think today about the legacy you're leaving behind for tomorrow. Love others, speak words of kindness, type words of edification, be slow to anger and celebrate each day, for none of us know what tomorrow holds and what folks will remember!

Hebrews 13:1 (KJV):

1Let brotherly love continue.

James 1:19 (KJV):

19 Wherefore, my beloved brethren, let every man be swift to hear, slow to speak, slow to wrath:

Romans 12:9-13 (ESV) :

Marks of the True Christian

9 Let love be genuine. Abhor what is evil; hold fast to what is good. 10 Love one another with brotherly affection. Outdo one another in showing honor. 11 Do not be slothful in zeal, be fervent in spirit, serve the Lord. 12 Rejoice in hope, be patient in tribulation, be constant in prayer. 13 Contribute to the needs of the saints and seek to show hospitality.

DEVOTION 25-WITH ME, ALWAYS

It's been an interesting morning! Today was our only day to sleep in this weekend and Maura, who was trying to take care of our sick dog by herself, woke us up at 7 a.m. Bless his heart, he was so sick. Bless her heart, she was trying so hard to be a good 'mother' and clean up after him.

Jeff and I got up and found the nearest coin laundry, counted up our coins and headed in with sheets, comforter and pillows. We waited while it washed for forty-five minutes, then went back in, loaded up the dryer and waited another twenty-eight minutes until all was clean. We came back to the bus, made up the bunk and finally crawled back into our own bed, when suddenly a scripture came to me about how the Lord is *always with me*...it was kind of comical thinking that He would be with me, even at the coin laundry, but that's what He promised, to be with me always!

Wherever you are today, at work, at home, in a hospital, or a cemetery, please remember that God is with you. You are never alone. I'm so grateful this morning to be reminded He is with me, always!

Psalm 139:8-10 (KJV):

8 If I ascend up into heaven, thou art there: if I make my bed in hell, behold, thou art there. 9 If I take the wings of the morning, and dwell in the uttermost parts of the sea; 10 Even there shall thy hand lead me, and thy right hand shall hold me.

Genesis 28:15 (ESV):

15 Behold, I am with you and will keep you wherever you go, and will bring you back to this land. For I will not leave you until I have done what I have promised you.

Matthew 28:20 (KJV):

20 Teaching them to observe all things whatsoever I have commanded you: and, lo, I am with you always, even unto the end of the world. Amen.

DEVOTION 26-AS GOOD AS IT GETS

A while back, I was talking with a friend about some things she was hoping would change in her life. She had been praying, but just didn't seem any closer to knowing what God's will was in this situation. I simply reminded her that if her life never changed from exactly the way it was this very moment, if this was as good as it gets, she'd have to be happy knowing this was God's plan for her life, otherwise she'd spend her whole life waiting for what was never going to be.

Many times, because it's hard to wait, we move forward without knowing God's direction only to find we're moving away from the plan He has purposed. Sometimes God is quiet, simply to remind us that waiting is necessary. He teaches us a lot about ourselves and about His faithfulness while we wait. Our job is to be patient, be quiet and trust Him to be all we need. When we do, this moment, the one in which we're living, is as good as it gets!

1 Samuel 13:8-14 (KJV):

8 And he tarried seven days, according to the set time that Samuel had appointed: but Samuel came not to Gilgal; and the people were scattered from him. 9 And Saul said, Bring hither a burnt offering to me, and peace offerings. And he offered the burnt offering. 10 And it came to pass, that as soon as he had made an end of offering the burnt offering, behold, Samuel came; and Saul went out to meet him, that he might salute him. 11 And Samuel said, What hast thou done? And Saul said, Because I saw that the people were scattered from me, and that thou camest not within the days appointed, and that the Philistines gathered themselves together at Michmash; 12 Therefore said I, The Philistines will come down now upon me to Gilgal, and I have not made supplication unto the Lord: I forced myself therefore, and offered a burnt offering. 13 And Samuel said to Saul, Thou hast done foolishly: thou hast not kept the commandment of the Lord thy God, which he commanded thee: for now would the Lord have established thy kingdom upon Israel forever. 14 But now thy kingdom shall not continue: the Lord hath sought him a man after his own heart, and the Lord hath commanded him to be captain over his people, because thou hast not kept that which the Lord commanded thee.

DEVOTION 27-PATCHWORK

I had a wonderful time last night with a lot of great friends. All of us are very different, yet we come together beautifully. We're all from different backgrounds, beliefs and cultures, we have different opinions and ideas, but we laugh at the same stories and when one of us hurts; we all hurt.

It reminded me of patchwork...quilts, tablecloths, and even shirts or pants, pieced together of hundreds of different patterns and textures, stitched to form a strong bond. Isn't that what the body of Christ is...individuals joining together because of our common belief in the power of the blood of Christ unto salvation? We must put aside our differences, trusting that our similarities will unite us; believing that the bonds that join us will be strong.

In your daily activities this week, notice the people that God has put in your path. Look at the differences you may have and learn from them, then, look at the similarities and celebrate the beauty of patchwork.

1 Corinthians 12:14-21 (ESV):

14 For the body does not consist of one member but of many. 15 If the foot should say, "Because I am not a hand, I do not belong to the body," that would not make it any less a part of the body. 16 And if the ear should say, "Because I am not an eye, I do not belong to the body," that would not make it any less a part of the body. 17 If the whole body were an eye, where would be the sense of hearing? If the whole body were an ear, where would be the sense of smell? 18 But as it is, God arranged the members in the body, each one of them, as he chose. 19 If all were a single member, where would the body be? 20 As it is, there are many parts, yet one body. 21 The eye cannot say to the hand, "I have no need of you," nor again the head to the feet, "I have no need of you."

1 Corinthians 12:27-31 (ESV):

27 Now you are the body of Christ and individually members of it. 28 And God has appointed in the church first apostles, second prophets, third teachers, then miracles, then gifts of healing, helping, administrating, and various kinds of tongues. 29 Are all apostles? Are all prophets? Are all teachers? Do all work miracles? 30 Do all possess gifts of healing? Do all speak with tongues? Do all interpret? 31 But earnestly desire the higher gifts. And I will show you a still more excellent way.

Romans 12:4-5 (ESV):

4 For as in one body we have many members, and the members do not all have the same function, 5 so we, though many, are one body in Christ, and individually members one of another.

Colossians 3:14-16 (ESV):

14 And above all these put on love, which binds everything together in perfect harmony. 15 And let the peace of Christ rule in your hearts, to which indeed you were called in one body. And be thankful. 16 Let the word of Christ dwell in you richly, teaching and admonishing one another in all wisdom, singing psalms and hymns and spiritual songs, with thankfulness in your hearts to God.

DEVOTION 28-THE PLAN

My girls' birthdays are only eleven days apart, which means we plan and participate in birthday celebrations for about two weeks in late September, and early October. We decide on cakes, ribbons, streamers, plates, cups, napkins, gifts, guest lists, and it just continues. Inevitably, something will be overlooked, and this year it was the lighter to light the candles during the birthday song. We finally found one to borrow and the party continued.

It just reminded me that all of the planning in the world couldn't stop the unexpected. Many of us feel like if we plan our lives, it will go according to plan...unfortunately, that's not the case. When we plan our lives, all we're doing is determining a path that may not be best for us, because we're unable to see what is ahead. It is better to draw closer to God, asking Him to lead and then trusting that He is giving us what is best.

Psalm 37:5 (KJV):

5 Commit thy way unto the Lord; trust also in him; and he shall bring it to pass.

Proverbs 16:9 (KJV):

9 A man's heart deviseth his way: but the Lord directeth his steps.

Matthew 6:33 (KJV):

33 But seek ye first the kingdom of God, and his righteousness; and all these things shall be added unto you.

DEVOTION 29-PICK IT UP!

I'm really disheartened and confused by so many of the statements I hear these days about preachers. If you open a newspaper or listen to the radio today, you might be confused about something I consider to be a basic knowledge about the Bible. The Bible explicitly says that God has provided the Holy Spirit to lead and guide us. It says that the knowledge of good and evil is placed within every man. Because this is true, why are so many these days in the media desperate to know a preacher's opinion on controversial matters? If the microphone were placed in your face, even if you were a preacher, why would your opinion matter...because it's just that; your opinion? And you're...just human.

I have been blessed to have some wonderful, godly men as my pastors through the years to teach me, lead me in a prayer of salvation, baptize me, marry me, and pray a prayer of dedication over all three of my children. I have been blessed. Yet I know many pastors who have had nervous breakdowns, battled demons of alcoholism, committed fraud, adultery and suicide. These men were human, living in an imperfect world as imperfect people. They had a heart's calling to serve God and delivered many thought provoking, illuminating messages during the course of their lives.

One of the greatest things you can do for your pastor is to pick up the Word of God and read it for yourself. There are over one hundred versions available and literally, hundreds of translations in English, hard back, leather back or online, and it even comes on CD; surely there is one for you. Your pastor spends time each week, visiting the sick, studying and preparing for his message, and praying for those who are hurting. The least you can do for him is to read the Bible for yourself and stop asking him to tell you what the Holy Spirit will if you'll take time to listen. This way, you're getting true and direct answers, instead of hearing from a secondary source.

Psalm 119:105 (NIV):

105 Your word is a lamp for my feet, a light on my path.

Psalm 119:11 (KJV):

11 Thy word have I hid in mine heart, that I might not sin against thee.

Joshua 1:8 (NIV):

8 Keep this Book of the Law always on your lips; meditate on it day and night, so that you may be careful to do everything written in it. Then you will be prosperous and successful.

Hebrews 4:12 (ESV):

12 For the word of God is living and active, sharper than any two-edged sword, piercing to the division of soul and of spirit, of joints and of marrow, and discerning the thoughts and intentions of the heart.

John 14:15-17 (ESV):

Jesus Promises the Holy Spirit

15 "If you love me, you will keep my commandments. 16 And I will ask the Father, and he will give you another Helper, to be with you forever, 17 even the Spirit of truth, whom the world cannot receive, because it neither sees him nor knows him. You know him, for he dwells with you and will be in you.

John 14:26 (ESV):

26 But the Helper, the Holy Spirit, whom the Father will send in my name, he will teach you all things and bring to your remembrance all that I have said to you.

DEVOTION 30-KEEPING IT REAL

I sing to an audience of real people with real problems. They are hurting and in need of a message of hope. If I stand on stage without compassion, without truly caring about them; I'm wasting valuable minutes of their time, and mine.

Sure, in any concert setting, it's important to make certain you give the best of your talents, and in any social setting, it's important to keep their attention by being funny or interesting. But by the end of the concert, it's important to me to leave something with them that they can carry in their hearts as they walk back into those very real problems.

My desire each night is to look into the eyes of hurting people and offer them my experiences hoping that they see the love and grace of Christ. Before you go out this week, take a few moments to read scriptures that encourage you. Prepare yourself to help a hurting world. Pray for the needs of your family and friends and ask God to fill you with His presence so that everyone you meet can experience Him. Someone you see will need you to keep it real!

Ephesians 3:16-21 (NIV):

16 I pray that out of his glorious riches he may strengthen you with power through his Spirit in your inner being, 17 so that Christ may dwell in your hearts through faith. And I pray that you, being rooted and established in love, 18 may have power, together with all the Lord's holy people, to grasp how wide and long and high and deep is the love of Christ, 19 and to know this love that surpasses knowledge—that you may be filled to the measure of all the fullness of God. 20 Now to him who is able to do immeasurably more than all we ask or imagine, according to his power that is at work within us, 21 to him be glory in the church and in Christ Jesus throughout all generations, forever and ever! Amen.

Ephesians 6:10-18 (ESV):

The Whole Armor of God

10 Finally, be strong in the Lord and in the strength of his might. 11 Put on the whole armor of God, that you may be able to stand against the schemes of the devil. 12 For we do not wrestle against flesh and blood, but against the rulers, against the authorities, against the cosmic powers over this present darkness, against the spiritual forces of evil in the heavenly places. 13 Therefore take up the whole armor of God, that you may be able to withstand in the evil day, and having done all, to stand firm. 14 Stand therefore, having fastened on the belt of truth, and having put on the breastplate of righteousness, 15 and, as shoes for your feet, having put on the readiness given by the gospel of peace. 16 In all circumstances take up the shield of faith, with which you can extinguish all the flaming darts of the evil one; 17 and take the helmet of salvation, and the sword of the Spirit, which is the word of God, 18 praying at all times in the Spirit, with all prayer and supplication. To that end keep alert with all perseverance, making supplication for all the saints,

DEVOTION 31-DIVINE APPOINTMENT

I heard a wonderful story this morning. We performed in a church that was awarded a Key to the City and a proclamation for their service during the community's time of need after a tornado had devastated the area last year.

The man spoke about what a divine appointment that was for his church. Then, he reminded the church that they didn't get that opportunity because they were the smartest church, or the most giving, or the best looking congregation...they received the opportunity simply because they were the only large building in the area that had lights, water, and power. They received a divine appointment because when the opportunity arose, they had what they needed and were ready to assist.

I loved that story. It just reminded me that if I stay in prayer, staying ready for what God may offer, I could be a help to someone else in need. I can have a divine appointment of my own if I am prepared and ready to assist...and it helps if I have the light of the world, the water of life, and power of God!

Hosea 10:12 (ESV):

12 Sow for yourselves righteousness; reap steadfast love; break up your fallow ground, for it is the time to seek the Lord, that he may come and rain righteousness upon you.

Colossians 4:2 (NIV):

Further instructions

2 Devote yourselves to prayer, being watchful and thankful.

Mark 13:33-37 (NIV):

33 Be on guard! Be alert! You do not know when that time will come. 34 It's like a man going away: He leaves his house and puts his servants in charge, each with their assigned task, and tells the one at the door to keep watch.

35 *"Therefore keep watch because you do not know when the owner of the house will come back—whether in the evening, or at midnight, or when the rooster crows, or at dawn.* **36** *If he comes suddenly, do not let him find you sleeping.* **37** *What I say to you, I say to everyone: 'Watch!'"*

DEVOTION 32-NO PLACE FOR ARROGANCE

There is simply no place for arrogance in the life of a Christian. According to the Bible, meekness, humility, love and service to others are the traits that you would be better to exhibit. If so, then why, when there are arguments about religion or politics, or any other controversial subject, do people who claim to be Christian, exhibit such arrogance and condescension?

When I was in Debate Club in high school, we were taught to back up our opinions with facts and I will admit that many times when I went into an argument to prove my opinion, by the time the fact finding was over, my opinion had changed. We were not allowed to speak down to our opponents, to belittle them or call them stupid, we were not allowed to raise our voices, no matter how passionate our feelings and we were to only present the facts and let the judge then determine the winner.

As Christian's when it comes to controversial topics; let's try more prayer, less talk, more facts, fewer opinions, and more meekness, respect and love for one another.

1 Samuel 2:3 (NIV):

3 Do not keep talking so proudly or let your mouth speak such arrogance, for the Lord is a God who knows, and by him deeds are weighed.

Romans 12:3 (ESV):

3 For by the grace given to me I say to everyone among you not to think of himself more highly than he ought to think, but to think with sober judgment, each according to the measure of faith that God has assigned.

Romans 14:1 (ESV):

1 As for the one who is weak in faith, welcome him, but not to quarrel over opinions.

DEVOTION 33-BOUNDARIES

I think the hardest part of being a parent is setting boundaries. Usually, when a child misbehaves, it's because they aren't
certain of how far you'll allow them to go. My children know
they've reached the end of my lenience when I begin counting
to three. They know it doesn't budge!

I'm beginning to believe that we, as Christians, need to be
reminded that we have better boundaries already set. We need
to remember the Ten Commandments; we need to remember
Jesus' commandment in the New Testament. As you read each
one, be honest with yourself. Ask yourself if you've blurred
some lines, allowed a little misuse of the definition. You need
boundaries and your heavenly Father knows that and has
already made provision!

Exodus 20:1-17 (MSG):

*1-2 God spoke all these words: I am God, your God, who
brought you out of the land of Egypt, out of a life of slavery.
3 No other gods, only me. 4-6 No carved gods of any size,
shape, or form of anything whatever, whether of things
that fly or walk or swim. Don't bow down to them and
don't serve them because I am God, your God, and I'm a
most jealous God, punishing the children for any sins their
parents pass on to them to the third, and yes, even to the
fourth generation of those who hate me. But I'm unswervingly loyal to the thousands who love me and keep my
commandments. 7 No using the name of God, your God, in
curses or silly banter; God won't put up with the irreverent
use of his name. 8-11 Observe the Sabbath day, to keep it
holy. Work six days and do everything you need to do. But
the seventh day is a Sabbath to God, your God. Don't do
any work—not you, nor your son, nor your daughter, nor
your servant, nor your maid, nor your animals, not even
the foreign guest visiting in your town. For in six days God*

made Heaven, Earth, and sea, and everything in them; he rested on the seventh day. Therefore God blessed the Sabbath day; he set it apart as a holy day. 12 Honor your father and mother so that you'll live a long time in the land that God, your God, is giving you. 13 No murder. 14 No adultery. 15 No stealing. 16 No lies about your neighbor. 17 No lusting after your neighbor's house—or wife or servant or maid or ox or donkey. Don't set your heart on anything that is your neighbor's.

John 13:34 (MSG):

34-35 "Let me give you a new command: Love one another. In the same way I loved you, you love one another. This is how everyone will recognize that you are my disciples— when they see the love you have for each other."

DEVOTION 34-THE VOICE OF GOD

I think one of the most asked questions regarding a relationship with Christ is; "How do I know what God is saying to me?" The Bible tells us that He speaks in a 'still, small voice'. It also says that some will 'have ears to hear' and that the 'sheep know the shepherd's voice.'

Although, I can't offer a definitive answer, I can tell you what I have done that gives me a greater confidence trusting that I am hearing the voice of God:

- I read His Word. Several years ago, I was given about twenty sample Bibles to review. When I asked about returning them, the clerk said to keep them or give them away to people who might need them. I gave away most of them, but kept three of four that were my favorites. I put them by my bed at home, in the bus, in the kitchen, and the office, that way wherever I was, there was a Bible within reach. Now, I even have an app on my phone. This way, I have constant access whenever there is a free moment to read.

- I pray constantly and I begin by saying thank-you! There's nothing like starting a conversation with gratitude for what you have, rather than asking for what you don't.

- I trust that He hears me and that He is leading and guiding me. The same way that I have to trust my husband when he says he loves me and has my best interests at heart, I also have to trust my relationship with God.

This week, pick up your Bible, read a few scriptures, then pause and thank God for His word. Ask Him to help you understand them and hear His voice more clearly.

1 Kings 19:12 (KJV):

*12 And after the earthquake a fire; but the Lord was not in the fire: and after the fire a **still small voice**.*

Ezekiel 12:2 (KJV):

*2 Son of man, thou dwellest in the midst of a rebellious house, which **have** eyes **to** see, and see not; they **have ears to hear**, and **hear** not: for they are a rebellious house.*

John 10:14 (KJV):

14 I am the good shepherd, and know my sheep, and am known of mine.

Romans 10:17 (KJV):

17 So then faith cometh by hearing, and hearing by the word of God.

2 Timothy 3:16 (KJV):

16 All scripture is given by inspiration of God, and is profitable for doctrine, for reproof, for correction, for instruction in righteousness:

DEVOTION 35-REFUSE THE NEWS

This week has been filled with bad news. Sometimes it feels like that's all we hear, and when it's all we hear; we become discouraged, fearful and ready to give up. I've decided to refuse the news!

First of all, turn off the television, turn off the radio, and turn off social media. Instead, look into the faces of the ones you love; or take a walk outside just to see and hear nature, open your favorite book, even if it's one from your childhood, turn on some Christmas music or a good old gospel song. Do this long enough for your heart to carry your head where it needs to be.

Secondly; say thanks. If you can't think of anything for which to be grateful, begin a list, starting with God's love, family, a roof over your head, physical and emotional warmth, a job, a car to drive to your job, two hands or two feet...this list will grow and soon you will be overwhelmed with your blessings.

1 Corinthians 9:24-25 (TLB):

24 In a race everyone runs, but only one person gets first prize. So run your race to win. 25 To win the contest you must deny yourselves many things that would keep you from doing your best. An athlete goes to all this trouble just to win a blue ribbon or a silver cup, but we do it for a heavenly reward that never disappears.

Romans 12:2 (TLB):

2 Don't copy the behavior and customs of this world, but be a new and different person with a fresh newness in all you do and think. Then you will learn from your own experience how his ways will really satisfy you.

Psalm 92:1-2 (KJV):

1 It is a good thing to give thanks unto the Lord, and to sing praises unto thy name, O Most High: 2 To shew forth thy loving kindness in the morning, and thy faithfulness every night,

Psalm 103:2 (KJV):

2 Bless the Lord, O my soul, and forget not all his benefits:

DEVOTION 36-INTENTIONALLY

This week, in the news and social media, I've noticed people complaining about EVERYTHING...even things completely out of their control like the weather. Yes, I've been guilty of the same, "It's just so cold", "Can you believe how cold it is?" and, "I just can't take anymore of this cold weather!" Only to say two months later, "It's so hot", "I don't think I can stand this heat another day!" We're Israelites, grumbling in the wilderness because we don't like manna!

On the surface, this seems so insignificant, unimportant, and we rationalize, "Everyone does it!" but that still doesn't dismiss the fact that it's negative and not a benefit to your attitude. I laughed this past spring and told my husband, "I've complained about the cold so much this winter, I'm not going to complain about the heat when summer comes!" I actually did pretty good and only complained a couple of times, do you want to know why? Because I committed to do so, to NOT complain about the weather, I decided instead to embrace it as a gift that I get to enjoy a variety of seasons.

Weather is just one kind of 'innocent' complaint that we allow ourselves, so examine the words you speak this week and see if any of them are the root of negativity and an enemy of your attitude! Look for these 'attackers' and stop them in their tracks by changing your thoughts and your words, intentionally! You *are* in charge!

Exodus 16:8 (NIV):

8 Moses also said, "You will know that it was the Lord when he gives you meat to eat in the evening and all the bread you want in the morning, because he has heard your grumbling against him. Who are we? You are not grumbling against us, but against the Lord."

Philippians 2:14 (ESV):

14 Do all things without grumbling or disputing,

1 Thessalonians 5:18 (KJV):

18 In every thing give thanks: for this is the will of God in Christ Jesus concerning you.

DEVOTION 37-SAYING GOODBYE

We buried Rudy, our ten year old Cocker Spaniel this week and our hearts were broken. He was a member of our family and each one of us grieved his death. We had a simple funeral; we held each other and we cried. We're a very close family and we saw the hurt in each other's eyes and offered comfort as best we could.

It made me think of all the other funerals I've attended, the family and friends I've mourned and the hurt and feelings of hopelessness that come with it all. I am grateful that my faith in God gives me hope for eternity.

Many studies have shown in grief; we all pass through five stages, denial, anger, bargaining (the "If only's"), sadness/regret, and finally acceptance. Although there is no method, we all pass through our own personal process of these stages.

If you are dealing with losses and grief, visit the scriptures and take comfort in the promises of God. These promises help us when we are required to say goodbye.

John 14:1-4 (KJV)

1 Let not your heart be troubled: ye believe in God, believe also in me. 2 In my Father's house are many mansions: if it were not so, I would have told you. I go to prepare a place for you. 3 And if I go and prepare a place for you, I will come again, and receive you unto myself; that where I am, there ye may be also. 4 And whither I go ye know, and the way ye know.

1 Thessalonians 5:9-11 (KJV):

9 For God hath not appointed us to wrath, but to obtain salvation by our Lord Jesus Christ, 10 Who died for us, that, whether we wake or sleep, we should live together with him. 11 Wherefore comfort yourselves together, and edify one another, even as also ye do.

John 11:23-26 (KJV):

23 Jesus saith unto her, Thy brother shall rise again. 24 Martha saith unto him, I know that he shall rise again in the resurrection at the last day. 25 Jesus said unto her, I am the resurrection, and the life: he that believeth in me, though he were dead, yet shall he live: 26 And whosoever liveth and believeth in me shall never die. Believest thou this?

Philippians 1:23-24 (KJV):

23 For I am in a strait betwixt two, having a desire to depart, and to be with Christ; which is far better: 24 Nevertheless to abide in the flesh is more needful for you.

Romans 8:38-39 (KJV):

38 For I am persuaded, that neither death, nor life, nor angels, nor principalities, nor powers, nor things present, nor things to come, 39 Nor height, nor depth, nor any other creature, shall be able to separate us from the love of God, which is in Christ Jesus our Lord.

Revelation 21:1-4 (KJV):

1 And I saw a new heaven and a new earth: for the first heaven and the first earth were passed away; and there was no more sea. 2 And I John saw the holy city, new Jerusalem, coming down from God out of heaven, prepared as a bride adorned for her husband. 3 And I heard a great voice out of heaven saying, Behold, the tabernacle of God is with men, and he will dwell with them, and they shall be his people, and God himself shall be with them, and be their God. 4 And God shall wipe away all tears from their eyes; and there shall be no more death, neither sorrow, nor crying, neither shall there be any more pain: for the former things are passed away.

DEVOTION 38-THE LOCKED DOOR

I had a wonderful conversation with an old friend this morning. His mother was a school teacher for over 30 years and whenever he says to me, "You know what my mama used to say..." my ears stand at attention because I know it's going to be good!

We were talking about raising children and how boundaries help children. They may not like them, but they need them desperately. This country needs boundaries. We don't need a 'yes' for every question we whine; the 'no's build character. If I had given my children a 'yes' for everything they asked of me; they would make terrible adults.

My friend explained it this way. His mama used to tell him that children are a lot like a police officer making his rounds of local businesses at midnight. The officer checks every door hoping it isn't open!

A child will walk through every open door, even the ones that may not be best for them, so as parents, don't be afraid to keep a few doors locked, even if you may lose a little popularity in doing so. Give your children boundaries that they so desperately need. And as an adult when a door is locked in front of you, trust that your heavenly Father knows what is best and sometimes that might be...a locked door.

2 Corinthians 6:14 (KJV):

14 Be ye not unequally yoked together with unbelievers: for what fellowship hath righteousness with unrighteousness? and what communion hath light with darkness?

Psalm 19:7-11 (KJV):

7 The law of the Lord is perfect, converting the soul: the testimony of the Lord is sure, making wise the simple. 8

The statutes of the Lord are right, rejoicing the heart: the commandment of the Lord is pure, enlightening the eyes. 9 The fear of the Lord is clean, enduring for ever: the judgments of the Lord are true and righteous altogether. 10 More to be desired are they than gold, yea, than much fine gold: sweeter also than honey and the honeycomb. 11 Moreover by them is thy servant warned: and in keeping of them there is great reward.

Joshua 1:8 (NIV):

8 Keep this Book of the Law always on your lips; meditate on it day and night, so that you may be careful to do everything written in it. Then you will be prosperous and successful.

Deuteronomy 28:1-6 (NIV):

Blessings for Obedience

1 If you fully obey the Lord your God and carefully follow all his commands I give you today, the Lord your God will set you high above all the nations on earth. 2 All these blessings will come on you and accompany you if you obey the Lord your God: 3 You will be blessed in the city and blessed in the country. 4 The fruit of your womb will be blessed, and the crops of your land and the young of your livestock—the calves of your herds and the lambs of your flocks. 5 Your basket and your kneading trough will be blessed. 6 You will be blessed when you come in and blessed when you go out.

DEVOTION 39-ALL TOO FAMILIAR

Sometimes we find ourselves all too familiar with the things of this life; in fact, we become ungrateful because we begin to take everything for granted. We forget what a precious gift our spouse and children are, we forget how blessed we are and we even forget that God loves us and that His Word is a light.

Ever found yourself groping in the darkness and realized that all you needed was a little light? I decided this week to re-examine five scriptures that I've heard all my life, five of the most popular Bible verses quoted. Read each of these, not quickly, not habitually, but contemplatively and deliberately. Let the words become a light for you in your darkness and remember to never allow them to become so familiar that they lose their ability to illuminate your life.

2 Timothy 3:16 (KJV):

16 All scripture is given by inspiration of God, and is profitable for doctrine, for reproof, for correction, for instruction in righteousness:

Romans 12:2 (KJV):

2 And be not conformed to this world: but be ye transformed by the renewing of your mind, that ye may prove what is that good, and acceptable, and perfect, will of God.

Proverbs 22:6 (KJV):

6 Train up a child in the way he should go: and when he is old, he will not depart from it.

Psalm 118:24 (KJV):

24 This is the day which the Lord hath made; we will rejoice and be glad in it.

Romans 8:28 (KJV):

28 And we know that all things work together for good to them that love God, to them who are the called according to his purpose.

DEVOTION 40-WHERE DO YOU LIVE?

I've been very blessed to meet some of my oldest, dearest friends during the thirty-six years that I've traveled and sang. These are friends who came to my graduation or wedding, who planned baby showers for me and who send me Christmas cards every year just to stay in touch. These are people from all over the country that if it were not for the music; I may never have known. I guess you could say they met me in the praises and presence of God.

I woke up excited this morning about getting to go to my own church. Because of the travels, I'm away often times and don't get to be with some of those precious friends like I would like to. But the love is always there, waiting for me when I get home. It made me start thinking about how important it is to my life, to live wrapped in the presence and praises of God. He promises to inhabit (to live in or occupy) the praises of His people. Where do you live? Do you live in his praises so that He will inhabit with you, or do you live in fears, doubts or complaints, alone in your misery? Offer Him praise this morning, sing a song of celebration and pray a prayer of gratitude, inviting God for a visit that will change your life.

Psalm 84:4 (KJV):

4 Blessed are they that dwell in thy house: they will be still praising thee. Selah.

Psalm 22:3 (KJV):

3 But thou art holy, O thou that inhabitest the praises of Israel.

Ephesians 5:19-20 (KJV):

19 Speaking to yourselves in psalms and hymns and spiritual songs, singing and making melody in your heart to the Lord; 20 Giving thanks always for all things unto God and the Father in the name of our Lord Jesus Christ;

DEVOTION 41-GET OUT OF THE BOAT

I think the hardest thing for me to do in my Christian walk is to face moments where I am required to step out of my comfort zone. When I am tossed into situations out of my control, it's easier for me to trust, because I know God has promised to be with me wherever I go, and I know His promises are true. But choosing to walk into the unknown is a little different, it requires faith in *your own ability* to seek and hear the voice of God.

When I am facing a difficult choice, I remind myself that God knows my struggle and will whisper my directions if I stay in constant communion with Him. I pray that God will open every door He wants me to enter and slam any door He doesn't. Don't even peek down the hallway that He doesn't want you to walk.

When you face choices, remind yourself of the depth of your relationship with God. Think of Peter, walking with your eyes on Christ alone, and just get out of the boat!

Matthew 14:22-29 (KJV):

22 And straightway Jesus constrained his disciples to get into a ship, and to go before him unto the other side, while he sent the multitudes away. 23 And when he had sent the multitudes away, he went up into a mountain apart to pray: and when the evening was come, he was there alone. 24 But the ship was now in the midst of the sea, tossed with waves: for the wind was contrary. 25 And in the fourth watch of the night Jesus went unto them, walking on the sea. 26 And when the disciples saw him walking on the sea, they were troubled, saying, It is a spirit; and they cried out for fear. 27 But straightway Jesus spake unto them, saying, Be of good cheer; it is I; be not afraid. 28 And Peter answered him and said, Lord, if it be thou, bid me come unto thee on the water. 29 And he said, Come. And when Peter was come down out of the ship, he walked on the water, to go to Jesus.

DEVOTION 42-CHALLENGE YOURSELF

It's funny how we are all guilty of settling in to a routine. Settling is sometimes good; remember, "A rolling stone gathers no moss?" Yes, we need to stay planted, but life is about change, the good and not so good. When we settle into a routine, we just go through the motions and we aren't really challenged to be better.

Every year, people make millions of resolutions, only to quit by the end of January. Why not instead, challenge yourself to simply do good things for yourself and others every week? Try keeping a journal listing one new thing weekly that you've never done before…by this time next year, you will have experienced fifty-two things you've never experienced. Volunteer with a local organization in your hometown, you'll meet lots of new friends and be a help to your community, too! Set goals and then, set out to accomplish them.

Whatever it is you choose to do, challenge yourself to be better, don't settle for less, when so much more is waiting for you!

Philippians 4:13 (KJV):

13 I can do all things through Christ which strengtheneth me.

2 Timothy 3:16 (KJV):

16 All scripture is given by inspiration of God, and is profitable for doctrine, for reproof, for correction, for instruction in righteousness:

Romans 12:1-2 (KJV):

1 I beseech you therefore, brethren, by the mercies of God, that ye present your bodies a living sacrifice, holy, acceptable unto God, which is your reasonable service. 2 And be not conformed to this world: but be ye transformed by the renewing of your mind, that ye may prove what is that good, and acceptable, and perfect, will of God.

DEVOTION 43-CHANGE

I'm always amazed when I see God working in my life or in the lives of my family and friends. It's not that I doubt His abilities, it's just that it's usually so perfectly designed that my tiny, little finite brain could never have come up with something so beautiful. That's when I simply have to stand back in awe to whisper, 'thank-you.'

Even though we know God is at work in our lives, change can still be very hard. You would think as much as life changes, we'd get used to it at some point, but it's just not so. We don't like change, even if we know it's going to be good for us. It's hard to let go of our comfort zones, even when our comfort zones are leading us nowhere.

So how do you adapt? How do you embrace change, rather than fight it? Pray for God's guidance. Admit to Him that you aren't able to do this alone. Find a scripture about change that encourages you and take a step in your new direction knowing that the One who never changes is leading you!

Malachi 3:6 (TLB):

6 For I am the Lord—I do not change. That is why you are not already utterly destroyed, for my mercy endures forever.

Hebrews 13:8 (KJV):

8 Jesus Christ is the same yesterday, and today, and forever.

Psalm 32:8 (NIV):

8 I will instruct you and teach you in the way you should go; I will counsel you with my loving eye on you.

Deuteronomy 31:8 (NIV):

8 The Lord himself goes before you and will be with you; he will never leave you nor forsake you. Do not be afraid; do not be discouraged.

Proverbs 3:5 (NIV):

5 Trust in the Lord with all your heart and lean not on your own understanding;

DEVOTION 44-KNEES

A friend told me last night, "I've been a lot of places, but the older I get I'm realizing that the best place for me to be is on my knees!" My grandma was a prayer warrior. It didn't matter where she traveled, her position of prayer was always the same. I watched her get down on her knees in hundreds of motel rooms, cabins on cruise ships, and especially in her home.

Last week I lay in my bed, anxious about many things. With an approaching cruise, deadlines to meet with our new project, Maura's school work, bills to pay for myself, our group and my Mama, my mind began to swirl out of control with one issue and then, another. It was 5:23 a.m. and I needed my rest. I began to pray, but somehow it felt like it was hitting the ceiling and no relief came. Immediately, I thought of Grandma and crawled out of bed, putting my knees on the floor and I poured out my heart to God, admitting I am simply not enough. I did my best and it wasn't good enough, so I asked Him to provide for me some tangible reminder that He was still in control. I asked Him for peace, so I could rest. God heard and answered.

If you're struggling with the weight of the world and having a hard time doing it all by yourself, why not give it to God? He loves you and wants you to trust Him with everything that burdens you. Like my grandma, I chose to seek Him on my knees.

Ephesians 3:14 (NIV):

A Prayer for the Ephesians

14 For this reason I kneel before the Father,

Acts 20:36 (NIV):

36 When Paul had finished speaking, he knelt down with all of them and prayed.

Luke 22:39-41 (NIV):

Jesus Prays on the Mount of Olives

39 Jesus went out as usual to the Mount of Olives, and his disciples followed him. 40 On reaching the place, he said to them, "Pray that you will not fall into temptation." 41 He withdrew about a stone's throw beyond them, knelt down and prayed,

DEVOTION 45-WEAR THE BADGE

Someone you meet today will have a story and his or her story could change your life. When you walk through unknown territory, it's comforting to know that someone has walked there before you and survived to tell about it. When I went through breast cancer, all I wanted to know is how someone else made it through. When my daddy died suddenly of a heart attack; I wanted to know how my friend, who had said goodbye to her mother a couple of years before, could ever smile again.

Don't be afraid to tell your story. Your story can change someone else's life. Sometimes it's hard because we fear our story labels us, but think of it this way…it actually puts a badge on us signaling to the world that we are overcomers. Don't be afraid to wear the badge. Whatever you have been through, whatever you have faced, share your story, the glory *and* the pain. Your story can help someone make it through.

1 Peter 3:15 (NIV):

15 But in your hearts revere Christ as Lord. Always be prepared to give an answer to everyone who asks you to give the reason for the hope that you have. But do this with gentleness and respect,

1 Chronicles 16:8 (NIV):

8 Give praise to the Lord, proclaim his name; make known among the nations what he has done.

Psalm 107:2 (KJV):

2 Let the redeemed of the Lord say so, whom he hath redeemed from the hand of the enemy;

DEVOTION 46-LOVE IS A CHOICE

Sometimes we forget love is a choice. We feel alone, neglected, cast aside and depressed because we don't feel like anyone loves us. We have to remember that love is a choice; we can choose to love, even when we don't feel loved.

Just like we can choose to be happy in the midst of tough situations, we can choose to love when we feel unlovable. The Bible says that we love God, because He first loved us. He *chose* to love us and now we can reciprocate that love and share it with others.

A friend of mine reminded me today that we have so much love to offer, to our spouse, our children, our parents, our friends and even strangers that we meet today. Offer a smile, a hug, or a cup of coffee to say to someone, I'm choosing to love!

1 John 4:19 (KJV):

19 We love him, because he first loved us.

John 13:34-35 (KJV):

34 A new commandment I give unto you, That ye love one another; as I have loved you, that ye also love one another. 35 By this shall all men know that ye are my disciples, if ye have love one to another.

1 John 4:7-12 (KJV):

7 Beloved, let us love one another: for love is of God; and every one that loveth is born of God, and knoweth God. 8 He that loveth not knoweth not God; for God is love. 9 In this was manifested the love of God toward us, because that God sent his only begotten Son into the world, that we might live through him. 10 Herein is love, not that we loved God, but that he loved us, and sent his Son to be the propitiation for our sins. 11 Beloved, if God so loved us, we ought also to love one another. 12 No man hath seen God at any time. If we love one another, God dwelleth in us, and his love is perfected in us.

DEVOTION 47-WORSHIP

Jeff and I were brought up in very different church settings. My church was quiet and reverent, and Jeff's was loud and joyful! We learned that worship could mean something to one person and something else totally to another. He likes to kid that even though we were brought up in different denominations, we're living proof that you can get along!

It made me start thinking this week, that as Christians, we shouldn't be so concerned with how we worship, but rather why we worship, because sometimes shouting worship will only work up a sweat and quiet worship can result in a nice nap! The 'why' makes all the difference!

We worship because we haven't forgotten what the hard times have taught us about God's faithfulness. We worship to say thank you Lord for the many blessings in our lives. We worship because we were created to do so! So worship with all of your heart, never forgetting why.

Psalm 95:6-7 (KJV):

6 O come, let us worship and bow down: let us kneel before the Lord our maker. 7 For he is our God; and we are the people of his pasture, and the sheep of his hand. To day if ye will hear his voice,

John 4:24 (KJV):

24 God is a Spirit: and they that worship him must worship him in spirit and in truth.

Psalm 8:1 (KJV):

1 O Lord, our Lord, how excellent is thy name in all the earth! who hast set thy glory above the heavens.

Psalm 118:1 (KJV):

1 O give thanks unto the Lord; for he is good: because his mercy endureth for ever.

Luke 4:8 (KJV):

8 And Jesus answered and said unto him, Get thee behind me, Satan: for it is written, Thou shalt worship the Lord thy God, and him only shalt thou serve.

DEVOTION 48-RESPECT

I believe that most every issue that we hear about these days can be traced back to the simplest of answers—a basic lack of respect, lack of respect for authority and lack of respect for one-self. People who live their lives without boundaries; sell themselves short. They never get the best of what life has to offer!

We are given rules, laws, and requests for obedience for our own good. No parent ever said to a child, "Do not cross the street without looking both ways" for their own good; it's for the child's safety. The Ten Commandments were given, not for God to show His authority, but for our own benefit. Accept His commandments in love and you will be blessed for it! Respect authority and respect yourself, trusting that the boundaries are set, not to *keep you from* good, but *for* your own good.

Exodus 20:1-17 The Message:

1-2 God spoke all these words: I am God, your God, who brought you out of the land of Egypt, out of a life of slavery. 3 No other gods, only me. 4-6 No carved gods of any size, shape, or form of anything whatever, whether of things that fly or walk or swim. Don't bow down to them and don't serve them because I am God, your God, and I'm a most jealous God, punishing the children for any sins their parents pass on to them to the third, and yes, even to the fourth generation of those who hate me. But I'm unswervingly loyal to the thousands who love me and keep my commandments. 7 No using the name of God, your God, in curses or silly banter; God won't put up with the irreverent use of his name. 8-11 Observe the Sabbath day, to keep it holy. Work six days and do everything you need to do. But the seventh day is a Sabbath to God, your God. Don't do any work—not you, nor your son, nor your daughter, nor your servant, nor your maid, nor your animals, not even the foreign guest visiting in your town. For in six days God *made Heaven, Earth, and sea, and everything in them; he rested on the seventh day. Therefore God blessed the Sabbath day; he set it apart as a holy day. **12** Honor your father and mother so that you'll live a long time in the land that God, your God, is giving you. **13** No murder. **14** No adultery. **15** No stealing.**16** No lies about your neighbor. **17** No lusting after your neighbor's house—or wife or servant or maid or ox or donkey. Don't set your heart on anything that is your neighbor's.*

DEVOTION 49-NO DISTRACTIONS!

Have you ever sat down with coffee in hand, ready to have your morning DEVOTIONal time with God and the phone rang or the pot on the stove boiled over? Maybe you've been out the door on the way to church and the car wouldn't start? These tiny distractions keep you from your much-needed time with God. Perhaps you tried to minister to, or encourage someone who was hurting, only to find yourself distracted by someone else's arguments, someone else's drama? I read a quote a few weeks ago that made me laugh; it read, "Not my circus, not my monkeys!"

Remind yourself of that the next time you are on a path that God has given you and you find one distraction after another trying to change your direction. Pray and ask God to keep you focused and keep your feet steady on the path that He is directing. If you're distracted by someone else's petty problems, you can't accomplish what God has called you to do... dismiss them as unimportant and move on to what *is* important, focus on God and His purpose for you!

Proverbs 4:25 (ESV):

25 Let your eyes look directly forward, and your gaze be straight before you.

Romans 8:35 (NIV):

35 Who shall separate us from the love of Christ? Shall trouble or hardship or persecution or famine or nakedness or danger or sword?

Romans 8:38-39 (NIV):

38 For I am convinced that neither death nor life, neither angels nor demons, neither the present nor the future, nor any powers, 39 neither height nor depth, nor anything else in all creation, will be able to separate us from the love of God that is in Christ Jesus our Lord.

Colossians 3:2 (ESV):

2 Set your minds on things that are above, not on things that are on earth.

Hebrews 2:1 (ESV):

1 Therefore we must pay much closer attention to what we have heard, lest we drift away from it.

DEVOTION 50-TAKE INVENTORY

I've been working all month getting my paperwork in order to file taxes. I've pulled copies of receipts, printed out pages of my general register, gathered important documents and started the process of looking back at what I did last year with every dollar that I earned. This way I'm keeping myself accountable.

Sometimes I'm impressed with how I've managed my spending, and sometimes I'm discouraged because I know I could have and should have done better. At times, it was easy finding certain items that were organized and placed exactly where they should have been filed, and every now and then, I had to search through mounds of paperwork to locate one receipt that was misfiled.

If I didn't have to pull all of this and organize my taxes year by year, and was required to wait until the end of my life assuming it was all as it should be; I'd probably be in big trouble. Somehow the unattended tiny mistakes add up to really big problems. It reminded me of how important a constant assessment of the way we live our lives is to the end result.

Some days I'm caring, I'm generous and wise, other days I'm quick tempered, self-centered and just plain dumb. Thank goodness I can read the Word of God and ask Him to show me where I've fallen short. I can pray for His strength to uphold me, His wisdom to guide me, and His peace to comfort me. Today, take inventory. Examine your heart and ask God to help you be accountable!

2 Peter 1:5-8 (ESV):

5 For this very reason, make every effort to supplement your faith with virtue, and virtue with knowledge, 6 and knowledge with self-control, and self-control with steadfastness, and steadfastness with godliness, 7 and godliness with brotherly affection, and brotherly affection with love.

8 For if these qualities are yours and are increasing, they keep you from being ineffective or unfruitful in the knowledge of our Lord Jesus Christ.

Romans 12:9-13 (ESV):

9 Let love be genuine. Abhor what is evil; hold fast to what is good. 10 Love one another with brotherly affection. Outdo one another in showing honor. 11 Do not be slothful in zeal, be fervent in spirit, serve the Lord. 12 Rejoice in hope, be patient in tribulation, be constant in prayer. 13 Contribute to the needs of the saints and seek to show hospitality.

DEVOTION 51-NO CHEATING ALLOWED!

Cheating is a word you don't hear used much among adults. Children are quick to tattle on someone who is cheating on a test, or cheating in a game, but somewhere between childhood and becoming an adult; we are sometimes guilty of looking the other way when a 'small' act of untruth slips by. Maybe it's because as adults, we witness such atrocities, that we forget that a 'little' cheat is still wrong in the eyes of God.

The Bible says that sin is sin, as Christians, we have the responsibility to be honest in all things and pure in all thoughts. The trouble with that is Christians were born into a world of sin, just like a non-Christians, so we battle against the same forces every day. What makes us different is the ability to be honest enough with ourselves, and with God to admit our shortcomings (our 'little' cheats) and do our best every day, thanking God for His grace when we simply aren't good enough!

When you feel tempted to manipulate a system to your favor, when you have the choice to keep secrets for your benefit, when you choose poorly by simply not choosing at all, think about how God will see your action. Will He see an act of purity, of goodness, of truth, or will He see an act of questionable character? Remember this whenever you are facing a choice and always remember, there's no cheating allowed!

James 4:17 (KJV):

17 Therefore to him that knoweth to do good, and doeth it not, to him it is sin.

DEVOTION 52-THE PLAN

This week's DEVOTION marks the ending of a three-year period of writing for me. As of this week, I have written one hundred fifty-six consecutive weekly DEVOTIONs and I have loved every minute of it. I have written when I was happy and sad, refreshed and tired, pleasant and irritable and a few hundred other adjectives describing my state of mind at the time of writing. I've written on Monday evenings with my due date seven days in front of me and I've written in the midnight hour on Sunday night, wondering if my lack of inspiration was taking up residence.

I've so enjoyed being able to put my heart into words and I'm grateful that while I've done that, God has used it to encourage others. I never planned to write weekly DEVOTIONs, I just started writing and God opened a door to share it with others. I also never planned to stop, but God is opening other doors and with our 30th anniversary approaching, a new project coming out in June and a many other responsibilities that come with it; I've decided that it may be time to take a break from weekly writing. The folks at Absolutely Gospel have told me that any time my heart has something to share, the platform will be waiting and for that I am so grateful! But for now, I'd like to leave you with a big thank-you for reading each week, and a reminder that this is a perfect example of life, beginnings and endings merging so closely that it's hard to decide which is which.

I choose to see it as a beautiful sunset on a warm summer day, and a stunning sunrise waking me up to what awaits, all wrapped up into one perfect plan orchestrated by the Master!

Ecclesiastes 3:1 (ESV):

1 For everything there is a season, and a time for every matter under heaven:

Proverbs 16:9 (ESV):

9 The heart of man plans his way, but the Lord establishes his steps.

Proverbs 19:21 (ESV):

21 Many are the plans in the mind of a man, but it is the purpose of the Lord that will stand.

Psalm 37:23 (NIV):

23 The Lord makes firm the steps of the one who delights in him;

Isaiah 14:24 (ESV):

24 The Lord of hosts has sworn: "As I have planned, so shall it be, and as I have purposed, so shall it stand,

Proverbs 16:3-4 (NIV):

3 Commit to the Lord whatever you do, and he will establish your plans. 4 The Lord works out everything to its proper end—even the wicked for a day of disaster.

TO CONTACT SHERI

P.O. Box 160
Lincolnton, GA 30817
www.jeffandsherieaster.com
Like her on Facebook, author page
Follow her on Twitter, @sherieaster

FOR BOOKINGS:

Beckie Simmons Agency
5543 Edmondson Pike #10
Nashville, TN 37211-5808
(615)595-7500
www.bsaworld.com

Other books by Sheri Easter, Hear My Heart, Xulon
Publishing, Copyright 2011, Eyes Wide Open Volume I,
Xulon Publishing, Copyright 2013, and Eyes Wide Open
Volume II, Xulon Publishing, Copyright 2014

To send a gift to The Lewis Family Homeplace, Inc.
P.O. Box 160
Lincolnton, GA 30817

MY PRAYER FOR YOU

Heavenly Father, because I have known Your goodness and Your mercy, may these words express the fullness of my heart so that the reader could find a deep-rooted joy and trust in You and You alone. Life can sometimes be very busy. I am grateful for a family who taught me Your words and Your promises. May I share them with those I meet each day, and may they see the witness in the works of Your hands. I am grateful for these and many more opportunities to allow others to live *Eyes Wide Open* with hearts full of gratitude, thanksgiving and praise.

Sheri Easter

"For God so loved the world, that he gave his only begotten Son, that whosoever believeth in him should not perish, but have everlasting life."

John 3:16 (KJV)

"For I am not ashamed of the gospel of Christ: for it is the power of God unto salvation to every one that believeth; to the Jew first, and also to the Greek."

Romans 1:16 (KJV)

"For whosoever shall call upon the name of the Lord shall be saved."

Romans 10:13 (KJV)

JEFF & SHERI EASTER

---◦∽◦⦿◦∾◦---

*A*fter thirty years of music and marriage, Jeff and Sheri continue to encourage hearts while setting a standard of excellence in the field of southern and country gospel music. Traveling now with their daughter Morgan on vocals, Jeff and Sheri have a dynamic sound/stage presence with unbelievable family harmonies and an authentic ability to communicate a message of hope.

For Jeff and Sheri, gospel music is genetically programmed into their DNA. As members of acclaimed musical families — Jeff's father is one of the Easter Brothers, and Sheri's mother is a member of the Lewis Family — they grew up surrounded by the sound of people praising God through their musical gifts.

In August of 1984, both were at the Albert E. Brumley Sundown to Sunup Gospel Singing in Arkansas. Jeff, who was playing bass for the Singing Americans at the time, took the opportunity to reintroduce himself to Sheri's mother, Polly; they had met on a previous occasion. Polly introduced Jeff to Sheri, and the two were married ten months later.

They traveled and performed as part of the Lewis Family for several years. But in 1988, they decided it was time to strike out on their own, and they haven't looked back since. Also joining Jeff and Sheri on the road is their daughter Morgan, who sings the harmonies, Maura Grace, their youngest daughter, who is a regular highlight of Jeff and Sheri's program, and cousin, Jared Easter on steel guitar, acoustic, mandolin and banjo, while Joshua Phillips plays drums.

Jeff and Sheri have been nominated for numerous Dove Awards and won seven. They've also received multiple Grammy nominations, and Sheri has been named Singing News Favorite Alto eleven times and the Singing News Female Vocalist four times, in addition she has claimed 21 multi-genre industry voted female vocalist awards. Jeff and Sheri's wall of awards also includes three Society for the Preservation of Bluegrass

Music Association Awards, two International Country Gospel Music Association Awards, nine Voice Awards for Christian Country Group, four Hearts Aflame Awards, and three Cash Box awards. They also have participated in the *Gaither Homecoming* video series since 1993, which have sold over 20 million units.

Apart from their frequent appearances on the Gaither Homecoming tour and videos, Jeff and Sheri have a fairly heavy touring schedule of their own. "When we perform, we want people to leave a little different than when they came in," Sheri explains. "We want them to have a great time smiling, laughing, crying, and healing. We want them to know God loves them and that He is in control."

ACCOMPLISHMENTS

Grammy Nomination (1992) Best Southern Gospel Album: *Pickin' the Best Live*

Grammy Nomination (2011) Best Southern, Country, or Bluegrass Gospel Album: *Expecting Good Things*

21st Annual Dove Award (1990) Country Album of the Year: *Heirloom*

30th Annual Dove Award (1999) Country Album of the Year: *Work in Progress*

33rd Annual Dove Award (2002) Country Recorded Song: "Goin' Away Party"

40th Annual Dove Award (2009) Bluegrass Recorded Song: "They're Holding Up the Ladder"; and Bluegrass Album of the Year: *We Are Family,* featuring the Lewis Family, the Easter Brothers, and Jeff & Sheri Easter

41st Annual Dove Award (2010) Southern Gospel Song of the Year: "Born to Climb"

42nd Annual Dove Award (2013) Country Album of the Year: "Eyes Wide Open"

Singing News Fan Awards (1991-1997, 2001, 2002, 2004, & 2008) Favorite Female Alto: Sheri Easter

Singing News Fan Awards (1995-1998) Favorite Southern Gospel Female: Sheri Easter

Singing News Fan Awards (2010) Horizon Individual: Morgan Easter

National Quartet Convention (2012-2013) Alto Singer of the Year: Sheri Easter

SGN Music Awards (2010) Musician of the Year: Madison Easter

Absolutely Gospel Music Awards (2011-2012) Musician of the Year: Madison Easter

Absolutely Gospel Music Awards (2012) Country Song of the Year: "Hear My Heart"

Absolutely Gospel Music Awards (2013) Country Album of the Year: *Eyes Wide Open*

Absolutely Gospel Music Awards (2014) Fan Favorite Artist of the Year and Special Event Project, *Like Father Like Son* (James & Jeff Easter)

Cash Box Awards (1989) Southern Gospel Female Vocalist and Southern Gospel New Female Vocalist: Sheri Easter; and Southern Gospel Duo of the Year

The Society for the Preservation of Bluegrass Music in America (1987, 1989, 1990) Female Vocalist of the Year, Contemporary: Sheri Easter

ICGMA (1994) Ms. ICGMA Georgia and Top Female Vocalist: Sheri Easter

The Voice (1990, 1992-1998, 2000) Female Vocalist of the Year: Sheri Easter

The Voice (1996-1997) Christian Country Group

The Voice (1994) Christian Country Song: "No Limit"

The Voice (1996) Christian Country Song: "Let the Little Things Go"

The Voice (1997) Christian Country Song: "Ever Since I Gave My Heart to You"

Gospel Line Fan Pick Awards (2001) Mixed Group

SGM FanFair/USGN Fan Awards (2006) Favorite Duet

SGM FanFair/USGN Fan Awards (2005, 2006) Favorite Alto: Sheri Easter

SGN Scoops Diamond Awards (2005, 2007, 2011, 2013) and Duet (2008) Female Vocalist: Sheri Easter

SGN Scoops Diamond Awards (2003) Bluegrass Gospel Artist

SGN Scoops Diamond Awards (2010) Christian Country Group of the Year and Bluegrass Gospel Artists of the Year; (2011) Mixed Group of the Year; (2012) Favorite Song, "Hear My Heart"

Southern Gospel News (2004) Special Event Project of the Year and Female Group of the Year: *Best of Friends*: Joyce Martin, Karen Peck Gooch, & Sheri Easter

Hearts Aflame Awards (1995) Album of the Year: *Thread of Hope;* and Song of the Year: "Thread of Hope"

Hearts Aflame Awards Concept Video of the Year: *Let the Little Things Go*

#1 Cash Box (November 18, 1989): "You'll Reap What You Sow"

#1 CCM Update Inspirational Song (June 7, 1989): "Prayer Warrior" *(Heirloom)*

#1 Southern Gospel Insight (June 10, 1991): "I Wonder If He Ever Cries"

#1 Christian Country (April-September 1993): "There Is a Way"

#1 CCM Christian Country: "Singing in My Soul"

#1 Gospel Voice (February 2001): "We're Not Gonna Bow"

#1 Power Source Christian Country (August 1999): "Been There, Done That"

#1 Southern Notes (December 1994): "Thread of Hope"

#1 US Gospel News: "Praise His Name"

#1 Singing News (February 2007): "Over and Over"; and (April 2010): "Born to Climb"

#1 Solid Gospel (2010) Song of the Year: "I Need You More Today"

In addition, over the past thirty years, Jeff and Sheri have produced over fifty Top 20 songs, received numerous Dove and Grammy Award nominations, and acquired various merits for outstanding character, humanitarian efforts, and charitable giving.

- Jeff & Sheri custom version of *The Adventure Bible*, Zondervan Bible Publishers (1991)

- Cover appearances on *Singing News, US Gospel News*, and *Homecoming* magazines

- Appearances on TNN's *Nashville Now,* Music City Tonight, The Grand Ole Opry, Trinity Broadcasting Network, Gospel Music Channel, Daystar, Inspirational Network and RFD-TV's The Marty Stuart Show, and Larry's Country Diner

- Appearance on the television series *Touched by an Angel,* "Shallow Water Part I & Part II" — Sheri in the role of Kay Winslow as part of Bill Gaither's Homecoming artists

- Regulars on Bill Gaither's *Homecoming* video series since 1993 and live tour dates since 1992

- Southern Gospel Music Association — Sheri Easter, board member

- Southern Gospel Songwriters' Association — Sheri Easter

- Sheri has authored three books, *Hear My Heart, Eyes Wide Open DEVOTIONal Series — Volume I & II*

- Hosts of INSP's series *Gospel Music Southern Style* (2010)

- Established The Lewis Family Homeplace Restoration Project and concert series, an organization honoring the legacy of The Lewis Family.

DISCOGRAPHY

1987 *New Tradition*

1988 *Homefolks*

1988 *Heirloom* (Sheri with Candy Hemphill Christmas and Tanya Goodman Sykes)

1989 *Picture Perfect Love*

1990 *Brand New Love*

1991 *Shining Through*

1992 *Pickin' the Best Live*

1993 *The Gift*

1994 *Thread of Hope*

1995 *Silent Witness*, and the compilation project *By Request*

1996 *Places in Time*

1997 *Sheri* (solo)

1998 *Work in Progress*

1999 *Sittin' on Cloud Nine*

2000 *Ordinary Day*, and the compilation project *Through the Years*

2001 *It Feels Like Christmas Again*

2002 *My Oh My*

2003 *Forever and a Day*

2003 *Best of Friends* (Sheri with Karen Peck Gooch and Joyce Martin)

2004 *Sunshine*

2005 *Miles & Milestones*

2006 *Life Is Great & Gettin' Better*

2008 *We Are Family* (Jeff & Sheri with the Easter Brothers & the Lewis Family)

2008 *Mayberry Live*

2010 *Expecting Good Things*

2010 *Live at Oak Tree Studios*

2011 *Silver* (A Twenty-Fifth Anniversary Celebration)

2012 *Eyes Wide Open*

2013 *Living With Eyes Wide Open*

2014 *Like Father Like Son* (James & Jeff Easter) and the compilation project *Yesterday*

2015 *Small Town* (Celebrating 30 Years of Music & Marriage)

Also available on eBook and Audio Book

CPSIA information can be obtained at www.ICGtesting.com
Printed in the USA
LVOW11s1931280815

451986LV00001B/21/P